C000021919

THE RIGH
KEEP CATS

THE RIGHT WAY TO KEEP CATS

Alison Wenlock

RIGHT WAY

Typeset in 11/12pt Times by One & A Half Graphics, Redhill, Surrey. Printed and bound in Great Britain by Cox & Wyman Ltd., Reading, Berkshire.

The *Right Way* series and the *Paperfronts* series are both published by Elliot Right Way Books, Brighton Road, Lower Kingswood, Tadworth, Surrey, KT20 6TD, U.K.

CONTENTS

1

CAT CULTURE

ORIGINS OF THE CAT

Although the cat is generally thought of as a domestic pet (and indeed it makes a very good one) it is in fact part of the family 'FELIDAE', which makes it a close relative of lions, tigers, and other wild cats. It is a distinguished family, dating back to the days of the first mammals, shortly after dinosaurs became extinct.

Even though you may think that your cat is very far removed from these wild and fierce creatures, every member of this family shares the same characteristics, seen in their behaviour towards each other, towards anything threatening and in their attitude to food and territory. Next time you watch a nature documentary on one of the big cats, try comparing the way a domestic cat behaves. You will see that there is really very little difference, once you take into account the variation in living environment.

The origins of the cat we now keep as a pet are not known for certain, but it is believed that it is descended from the original Egyptian wild cat, 'Felis Lybica'. This cat probably cross-bred with 'Felis Sylvestris', the British wild cat, to develop eventually into the domestic cat we know and love today.

UNDERSTANDING CAT CULTURE

Cats are very independent, proud creatures. They are also capable of giving great affection to their owners. However, because of their independent streak and the fact that they are often not as vocal as, for example, dogs are, they are often misunderstood. Yet the clues are always there for us to see in their behaviour and their body language, not to mention the wide range of sounds which form part of a cat's natural speech. All we have to do is watch, listen and interpret them correctly.

Cat Speech

If asked to describe a cat's speech, most people would describe a 'purr' or a 'miaow', but in reality there is far more to the average cat's repertoire than just these two sounds. Much of cat speech is related to particular events in the cat's life. For a start, there is the happy little chirrup which a cat will make to greet its owner; probably as near to 'hello' as a feline voicebox can manage.

Secondly, there is a peculiar clicking sort of noise which a cat will make in its throat when it can see prey of some kind. You may hear a cat do this when it can see birds up in a nearby tree, or even outside a window.

A cat makes this type of noise rather than a full-scale miaow for two reasons. The first is that it is a very different noise from the rest of its speech, and so is easy to distinguish and recognise; the second is that it is much quieter than a full-scale miaow would be. Both of these are very important when hunting prey. The cat needs to alert any other cats in the area that it has located prey and does not want the prey to be disturbed, or to be interrupted itself. Equally, it cannot afford to make a noise so loud that it will alert the potential prey and so allow it to escape.

Types of Miaow

The miaow itself comes in many different varieties. There is a short, high-pitched miaow, usually repeated, which the cat uses when it is looking for its owner, generally whilst on the move. Next there is the demand miaow, which is used to ask for something, for example for a door to be opened. This usually starts at medium pitch and volume, but becomes louder and more insistent if the request isn't quickly granted.

If the demand miaow is accompanied by a tail held straight

up in the air and determined eye contact, then it is a very serious request indeed (usually for food), and will be repeated with great insistence and volume until satisfied.

There is also a protest miaow in the cat's vocabulary and this can be used to indicate something with which it is not happy (such as being picked up and moved) or some kind of disruption to its routine. This sound is often used when furniture has been moved to a different location, or when the cat's bed or food dishes have been shifted to somewhere new. (It is always advisable to show your cat the new location when you have moved its dishes or bed, otherwise you will run the risk of it standing in the previous place and giving full vent to a protest miaow until you do.)

The protest miaow becomes a full-blooded yell of fury when your cat is confined, for example in a cat basket. It will sound as if your cat must be in excruciating pain, but don't be tempted to open the basket to check; your cat is just angry. If you let it out of the basket, you will have a very difficult job in catching it again. Cats are not silly enough to let themselves be easily caught twice in a row.

Other Sounds

If your cat really is in pain, for instance if someone accidentally treads on its tail, it will make a noise which sounds much more like a scream, shorter and at a much higher pitch. If it is in considerable pain, for example from an internal injury of some kind, it may either make no noise at all or it may make a soft purr. This purr does *not* mean that it is happy in these circumstances; it is just the cat's way of coping with the pain.

Other types of calling miaow may also be made in communication with other cats or sometimes different animals such as dogs. These calls usually result from two sources: aggression and fear. A cat will often miaow with its mouth open and teeth bared to intimidate a rival.

On occasions it may spit as well, usually accompanied by an

arched back and bristling fur, all designed to terrify the opposition. It may also do this when faced with a really frightening enemy such as a large dog, and will often retreat to as high a position as it can find, from where it will make the threat gestures.

When it has just completed a fruitful hunt, the cat may also produce a very loud, deep miaow. This is a way of announcing its success to the world.

The Contented Purr
At times of extreme relaxation and happiness, such as when it is being stroked by its owner, a cat will often make small murmuring sounds, indicating pleasure. These will sometimes develop into a deep purring sound, as contentment increases. The volume and pitch of the purr varies greatly between cats, with some purring much more readily than others.

Body Language
A cat's body language is absolutely fascinating and once you have started to observe it, you will find that it gives you all sorts of hints about how the cat is feeling. In actual fact a cat will tell you far more through its postures and movements than it ever will through the sounds it makes, so it is well worth studying. As well as the obvious things such as how it stands or lies down, a cat will tell you a vast amount through the use of its eyes, ears, mouth and tail.

What you can tell from a Cat's Eyes
The first thing to notice is how wide open the eyes are, because this will tell you how alert the cat is. If it is happy and relaxed, completely free from anxiety about anything, the cat's eyes will often be half-closed. If it is completely relaxed, it will often close its eyes, although it may not in fact be asleep. As it becomes more alert, so it will open its eyes wider.

The next indicators to look at are the pupils of the eyes. As well as the changes to the pupils brought on by the light

Fig. 1. *Left:* **Cat's face with dilated pupils.**
Right: **Cat's face with contracted pupils**

(enlarged in dim light, contracted in bright light), the pupils also change with the mood of the cat. When it is frightened by something the pupils dilate, becoming round black circles. If it is angry, they contract into narrow black slits.

What you can tell from a Cat's Ears
A cat's ears will always mirror its mood, and watching them will tell you a lot about how the cat is feeling. A cat's ears are rarely still, because even when it is relaxed it will still be monitoring any noises, just in case something interesting might happen. The ears will usually twitch in response to a noise and if the cat becomes more alert, they will be pricked forward. A cat who is on the prowl, or out hunting, will automatically keep its ears pricked the whole time.

If your cat becomes nervous for any reason, then its ears will start to twitch backwards. If something really frightening happens, then its ears will be completely flattened against its head, and it will probably assume a low, crouched position.

What the Cat's Mouth will tell you

A cat with its teeth bared, hissing and spitting, can be quite a frightening sight (and it is meant to be so). The cat is trying to make itself look terrifying, with the aim of warning the opposition not to make an attack.

If your cat has dilated pupils, flattened ears, bristling whiskers and an open mouth baring its teeth, then it is frightened and preparing for an attack. It may also twitch its tail, and crouch down, ready to defend itself, probably also making a great deal of aggressive noise.

The cat's mouth can indicate its temper, as well as showing fear. A disgruntled cat will always show this through its mouth. If it is finding something or someone disagreeable, it will clamp its jaws together and produce a tightly-closed mouth shape which can best be described as sulky. The whiskers will also be drawn forward more than usual, emphasising the effect.

Anxious cats, especially kittens, will also display this emotion through their mouths, which are generally kept open to the accompaniment of considerable distress miaowing until the source of the problem is dealt with.

What you can tell from the Tail

A cat's tail is a good indicator of its mood, but you have to be able to monitor the *degree* of tail movement to be able to interpret it correctly. For example, a small swish at the very end of the tail indicates pleasure and contentment. (Your cat may well do this when it is lying down and you are stroking it.)

Beware, though, if the swishing of the tail becomes a stronger twitch and the whole tail is swung from side to side – this means that the cat is getting very irritated by whatever you are doing. If you ignore this warning sign then your cat may give you another 'stop' message, such as a playful nip with its teeth. A more developed form of this can be seen in a cat which is about to launch an attack, and when this happens the whole tail will thrash from side to side.

A happy cat will normally carry its tail quite high, especially when running to greet you after an absence of any kind, or in anticipation of being fed something tasty. At times of particular delight the tail will be held straight up in the air.

Territory

Cats are extremely territorial creatures and spend much of their lives establishing, patrolling and defending their territory. It is partly for this reason that they become upset when they have to move house, travel away from home, or when their territory is changed by their owners. Even a small change, such as the addition of a bench or a garden pond, will stimulate large amounts of interest and comment from the resident cat.

A cat's territory will usually consist of its own house and garden, plus an additional part of the surrounding area. The size of this additional area will vary depending on a number of different factors. Firstly, it will depend on how many other cats live in the surrounding area (and who will therefore dispute the territory). The more there are, the smaller the individual territory they will each establish.

If there is more than one cat living in a particular house, then generally the cats will also divide up the house between them, with shared areas into which they are both allowed, such as the room where they are fed and the access to the catflap or outside door. If there is no cat living in a certain house, then it will form part of the territory of any other local cat willing to stake a claim to it, or it may even be shared between more than one.

Territorial Behaviour

For the above reason, when a new cat moves into the area, it will always have to establish its territory afresh, usually through disputes and fights with those cats already claiming it. If you have recently moved house, or recently acquired a cat, and it comes home with scratches on its nose, then it has probably been establishing its territory in the time-honoured fashion.

A tom cat will always try to establish a much larger territory than a female, or a neutered cat, for the simple reason that he will need to wander further afield to find a mate. This means that he has a larger territory to defend and so must spend that much more time away from his home base, often having to fight more territorial disputes than a neutered cat would.

Once established, territorial boundaries are not permanently fixed and are open to dispute at any time. If a cat becomes weaker through illness or injury, or if a larger, more aggressive cat moves in next door, then it may have to relinquish some of its hard-won territory.

Patrolling and marking the territory form a very important part of the cat's daily routine. It will rub its face, body and tail regions over various parts of the territory, particularly boundary areas, in order to leave its scent on them, warning off potential intruders.

You may notice that your cat will also enjoy sitting up somewhere high, from where it has an excellent view of any movement within the territory. This acts as an early warning system, and also gives it an added advantage in any fights which may occur. The cat which has the high ground is almost always the dominant one, since it is much easier to defend from above. Quite often a challenge from another cat can be dismissed by use of eye contact and threat gestures from the cat holding the higher ground. The challenger may then simply back off and a fight can be avoided.

Hunting
Hunting is an extremely strong instinct in most cats, whether they are fed well by you or not. The urge to hunt can be seen in kittens from an early age, as they play at stalking and pouncing, and they are often trained in this by their mother. It is simply in their nature, and is something which we must accept. It is entirely useless to try to stop them, and cruel to punish what is a perfectly natural part of their behaviour.

If you shout at your cat for bringing back a mouse then the

cat will just end up confused. When it brings its kill home to you, it is really rewarding you for feeding it, in the same way as its larger cousins will share their kills with each other in the wild.

It is best just to accept it, dispose of the kill and give your cat some other food to replace it. Most kills will appear intact, but unfortunately sometimes the cat will eat these before you can get to them, leaving just the grisly remains behind. It can be upsetting to see this, particularly for children, but it *is* part of nature and often it is the weaker and slower birds and rodents which get caught. This is part of the process known as 'natural selection' which ensures that the strongest survive.

It helps to remember that the majority of your cat's attempts to kill will be unsuccessful, because the odds are normally stacked in favour of the intended prey. This is especially true in the case of birds, where the potential victim will usually fly off to the nearest tree and scold the cat from a safe height.

Precautions you can Consider
A collar with a bell does sometimes alert birds in time for them to escape a stalking cat, but many cats may not accept a bell and will go berserk trying to remove the collar. Also, with any collar there is a risk that it will get caught when a cat is climbing and strangle the cat, so it is not without its own problems. (If you do decide to put a collar on your cat, make sure it is an elasticated one to lessen the risk.)

Most cats will from preference hunt at night, so if you can persuade yours to stay in at night, it may reduce the number of kills it brings home. If you secure the catflap at night, it will prevent your cat from thoughtfully bringing your share of the night's kill straight into the house for you. It can be very unpleasant to be confronted with a dead bird or rodent first thing in the morning.

Cats will often chase insects such as bees, butterflies and spiders, although they rarely catch them. If cats have access to a pond, they may also chase frogs and try to catch fish, although some cats are content simply to lie by the pool and watch the fish play. Most cats have a great dislike of water, so will try to avoid getting wet, which rather spoils their ability as fishermen. If you discover that your cat is poaching the fish from your pond, then either raise the perimeter boundary by building a wall or similar around it (if this will fit in with the landscaping) or fit a piece of light steel mesh over it. Both should prevent the cat from being able to fish in the water with its paws.

Grooming

Cats are naturally very clean animals and grooming forms a major part of their daily routine. They will clean themselves from top to toe using their own saliva and licking every part of their bodies. If they cannot reach a particular part, then they will lick their paws and use these to give themselves a good wipe over.

Grooming removes any loose or matted hair, or flakes of dead skin from the cat's coat, and keeps the fur in good order. If there are any small knots or burrs in the fur, then the front teeth may be gently used to tease these out. The action of licking the fur allows the cat to take in vitamin D which has been produced by sunlight acting on the coat, and the evaporation of saliva also has a cooling effect. This is especially important in the hot weather, since the cat has no sweat glands on the main parts of its body to help it to cool down.

Grooming also reinforces the bond between some cats; for example, kittens from the same litter may groom each other. Mothers will spend a lot of time grooming their kittens and adult cats living in the same house may also groom each other as a way of cementing their friendship.

Sleeping

Cats seem to spend more time sleeping than any other mammal, often breaking up their sleep into a number of quite lengthy naps. Generally they will find a warm, safe spot and curl up into a tight little circle, sometimes with the paws over the head. A period of light dozing will follow, usually for half an hour or so, which may then be followed by a period of deep sleep lasting several hours if the cat is not disturbed.

Although kittens begin life by sleeping next to each other for warmth and companionship, generally by the time a cat reaches adulthood it prefers to sleep by itself. It may spend large portions of the day asleep, being more active in the early morning and evening, which are the best times for hunting. Both younger and older cats tend to sleep even more than usual.

After sleeping, the first thing a cat will do is to arch its back and stretch its spine, usually accompanied by a big yawn. This gets its circulation working and its body back into shape for the next period of activity. Often it will be followed by a quick wash before the cat sets off to patrol its territory.

Playing

Play forms a vital part of the cat's development, through which it learns most of the skills it will need throughout its life. In particular, it will learn to stalk, pounce and kill, in order to hunt successfully. It will practise all the moves it requires using its brothers and sisters or its long-suffering mother as targets.

If you provide your kittens with a toy such as a ball or a catnip mouse, they will treat it as if it were real live prey. Once they have captured it, they will eventually pick it up in their mouths and carry it back to their bed, just as a wild cat would take its kill home to its den. A kitten will also learn how to defend itself through practice with its brothers and sisters, again trying out threat gestures, sparring and submissions, until it has perfected them.

However, although it will have learned these skills by the time it is an adult, a cat will still enjoy a good game if it gets the chance. Grown-up cats will often play hide and seek or chase with each other, and will happily play with you if you are prepared to dangle a piece of string in the air, or drag a stick across the ground for them to chase and pounce on.

Fighting

Although cats are normally quite aggressive creatures and disputes over territory can be frequent, full-scale cat fights are really quite rare. They do their best to avoid inflicting injuries upon each other, except when they are forced to for the sake of survival.

This can be seen in the case of kittens practising their combat skills through play fighting. They can often seem to be quite rough with each other, but they rarely bite hard and so injuries are very unusual. The same rule still applies later in life when there is a dispute between adult cats.

The conflict will generally begin with threat gestures from both cats, at which point one will probably back down and slink away. Usually the larger or stronger of the two will win without having to strike a single blow, simply because it looks more fierce. However, if the two appear equally matched and neither is prepared to give way, then a real fight may take place.

Fighting is usually not prolonged; in most cases a few blows are struck and the cats will break apart again. This scenario may be repeated once or twice, until a winner emerges. Generally it is all over quite quickly, without too much damage to the loser, although sometimes cats can receive nasty bites which can turn septic if untreated. If your cat does receive a deep wound, then it is better to let your vet have a look at it.

2

ANATOMY OF
THE CAT

SKELETAL STRUCTURE

All cats are superb athletes, and the major reason for this is their marvellously flexible skeleton. A cat can jump and twist with remarkable ease, as well as turn itself right around during a fall to make sure that it lands on its feet. It can run at great speed almost silently, which is a great asset when catching prey, and although it cannot run at this pace for long periods of time, it is certainly fit enough to overtake most creatures it wants to catch. Equally, its speed can save it from danger; often

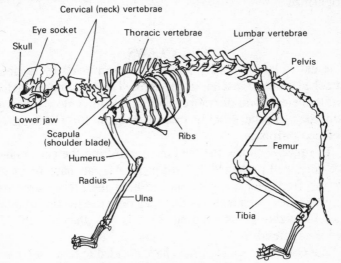

Fig. 2. The skeleton of a cat.

a fast sprint to the nearest tree will get it out of trouble. This is very useful when there is a large dog on its heels.

There are more than two hundred and forty bones in a cat's body, with twenty-one in the tail alone. This helps to explain how a cat can manoeuvre itself into so many different (and apparently awkward) positions. The longest bone in the cat's body is the shin bone, or 'tibia', and it is from the cat's hind legs that most of its power and speed comes. Unlike most other mammals which move their legs in opposite pairs (left front and right rear, then right front and left rear), when it is running the cat moves its front legs together, followed by its back legs. The front legs give direction and stability, but the hind legs inject the power and speed into its performance.

The cat has a remarkably mobile shoulder joint, which means that it has a great deal of flexibility in its front legs and can move these easily in various directions. The spine is also very flexible, which explains why the cat can twist so easily and curl itself up into a relatively small space. It also explains how it can arch its back to such a considerable extent when frightened.

THE CLAWS

The cat's claws are very strong and are moved by tendons attached to the muscles in the toes. They can be retracted while the cat is on the move so that they don't slow it down, and they can be quickly extended again for climbing or defence purposes.

To prevent injury, the tendons controlling the cat's claws are very well protected by hard pads. All cats have five toes on the front feet and four on the hind feet. They are also 'digitigrades', which means that they only use the tips of their toes for walking and running. This is why they are able to move so silently.

In recent years some owners have decided to have their cat's front claws surgically removed. This is a revolting practice,

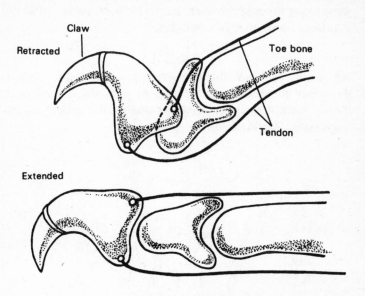

Claw

Retracted

Toe bone

Tendon

Extended

Fig. 3. *Above:* Cat's claw retracted.
Below: Cat's claw extended.

causing discomfort to the cat, as well as making it very difficult for it to climb adequately because it uses its claws to grip with. Equally, without its front claws to defend itself, it is left at the mercy of any other animal which chooses to attack it. If your cat's scratching is a problem, then it is better to train it to scratch outside the house, or else invest in a scratching post. Maiming your pet by removing its claws is not the right solution.

MUSCLES

Cats have more than five hundred highly developed muscles in their bodies, which give them a surprising amount of strength

for their small size, not to mention amazing agility. A cat can
jump many times higher than itself with no apparent difficulty,
thanks to these powerful muscles.

TEETH

An adult cat has thirty sharply-pointed teeth, suitably
developed for catching and eating its prey and for defending
itself. There are sixteen teeth located on the upper jaw and
fourteen on the lower one.

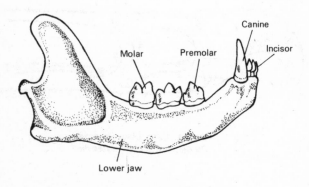

Fig. 4.   The lower jaw, showing the teeth.

The incisor teeth are small, and the four canine teeth are long
with a sharp inner edge for cutting. In some cases the molars
have been found to have as many as five sharp points on them.
The teeth are very hard and are perfectly adapted to the needs
of a cat living in the wild, but because of this they can
deteriorate and decay if a cat is fed solely on soft, tinned cat
food. It is advisable also to give your cat some of the crunchy,
dry cat food which is now available, to supplement its diet and
keep its teeth in good condition.

THE TONGUE

The under part of the tongue is soft and smooth, while the upper part is rough and covered with tiny hooks. These hooks cover the middle of the tongue, with the extreme back and sides being covered with taste-buds instead. The hooks are used to grip the cat's prey, but they are also useful for grooming purposes, because they can help to remove any debris from the coat.

When the cat takes in liquid, the tongue curls up at the end to form a cup shape, allowing the cat to lap very efficiently. The taste-buds are very well developed and the cat is therefore extremely sensitive to flavours. For this reason it may sometimes be a fussy eater, especially if its usual diet is suddenly changed. It can also easily detect food which is starting to go off and will not touch this. Neither will it happily drink water which is not pure.

THE MAJOR ORGANS AND NORMAL HEALTH

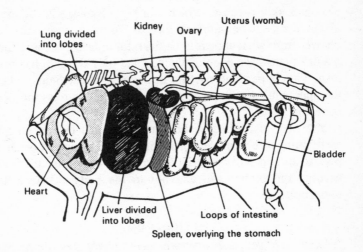

Fig. 5. The major organs.

The average cat weighs about 3.6kg (8 lb), with the normal range being 2.7kg − 6.3kg (6 lb − 14 lb), depending on age and breed.

The pulse rate (which can be taken by feeling for the pulse beat on the left-hand side of the rib cage or by pressing into the groin to detect the main thigh or 'femoral' artery) is normally about 110.

A cat's temperature should be at about 38 degrees Centigrade (101 degrees Fahrenheit) and it should not vary more than a degree from this. If it goes up suddenly consult your vet, because this could be a sign of serious illness. The temperature is normally taken by inserting a thermometer gently into the rectum, but this can be tricky as most cats will try to resist attempts to do this. If possible, one person should be available to restrain and soothe the cat while the other takes the temperature. If it is proving too difficult, don't risk injury to your cat; instead ask your vet to check the temperature for you.

THE SKIN

The cat's skin is loose, which is a big advantage in the event of any accident or injury to the cat. In many cases cats can recover from what appear to be frightful injuries, because their major organs have been untouched and only the skin has been torn. This is particularly true in the case of cat fights, where the opponent's teeth may fasten on the skin and miss the flesh beneath.

You may also observe how a mother cat can fasten her teeth quite safely on the scruff of a kitten's neck in order to pick it up and move it; this is simply because her teeth are holding on to the skin and not to the body of the kitten underneath it.

WHISKERS

All cats have very sensitive whiskers, which they use to help them to balance and to judge distances. There are special nerve endings in the whiskers to enable them to be used in this way and for this reason they should *never* be trimmed. A cat with damaged whiskers may become disorientated and confused. Most cats have about twelve whiskers on each side of their mouth with additional ones over their eyes and on the sides of their heads.

THE FIVE SENSES

Like any natural hunter, the cat needs to rely very heavily upon its senses, and for this reason they are very finely developed. Kittens take a while to use their senses fully; for example they do not have a proper awareness of height when young and so should be kept away from high, open windows. They may also be slightly clumsy at first, taking a while to reach their full agility and natural sense of balance.

Sight

A cat's sight is extremely effective, in all types of light, including darkness. It has special cells in its eyes which can reflect back any available light on to the retina, so that it can see dimly even when there is next to no light. This feature also makes its eyes appear to glow strangely in the dark, no doubt part of the reason why people were traditionally so superstitious about cats.

Looking at a cat's face, you will be able to see that its eyes are positioned on either side of the head, in such a way as to give overlapping vision. This means that a cat can be very accurate about distance and speed, so not only can it easily calculate where its prey is, it can also jump large distances accurately and land with no risk of missing its footing.

Sense of Smell

Cats rely a great deal on their sense of smell, which is much more accurate than ours. From the day it is born, a kitten will orientate itself guided by smell alone. It will judge where its mother is by her smell, and will be able to distinguish its brothers and sisters by theirs. As it grows up, it will learn to recognise the smell of its owner and all the special odours which can be found in the house where it lives. It will also detect whether other cats have been visiting its territory by the smell which they have left behind.

You may notice that your cat will show a particular interest in shoes or boots; this is because they still retain the smell of all the fascinating places they have been walking in. In the same way, a cat will often sniff the family car after it returns home from a trip because it smells strange.

Equally, any new furniture or household item will have a different, foreign smell and is likely to cause your cat to give it a good sniff. The same treatment may be given to any visitor coming in to the house, and in fact the best way for new people to make friends with your cat is to offer it a hand to sniff. If it likes the smell, it will probably be quite happy to allow them to stroke it. However, if they own a large dog or another cat, do not be too surprised if your cat is not at all friendly towards them; it will be able to smell the scent of the other animal.

In fact, anything new in the cat's life is usually greeted with a sniff first, because this is a major way of collecting information for cats. You will probably notice that food is always sniffed before tasting, and anything remotely suspect is ignored.

Sense of Taste

Like us, cats really do enjoy their food and their palates can become jaded if they are given too much of the same thing. This can lead to increasing fussiness about what they will and will not eat. Unfortunately cats can be extremely stubborn about this, being willing to starve rather than touch food which they consider to be unappetising.

The best way of dealing with this is to vary the flavours and textures which you feed your cat, so that it doesn't get bored with the taste. If there is a food which it obviously dislikes, try something else. You are unlikely to be able to persuade it to eat through hunger.

Even though you may be feeding it well and it is enjoying its food, a cat will still nibble the odd piece of grass or cat mint for simple enjoyment of the taste. This is not harmful, and although a cat may sometimes be sick if it eats too much grass, there are generally no lasting ill effects.

Hearing

Like the other senses, a cat's hearing is very acute. Cats can hear all sorts of sounds which humans miss, particularly high-pitched ones which are out of our range. This helps them to find their prey because they can hear small sounds in the undergrowth from quite a distance away.

Cats are also very clever at distinguishing between similar noises, such as cars and footsteps. It is quite common for a cat to respond only to its owner's footsteps or car engine, even though it may be hearing similar noises all day long. In the same way, a cat will soon learn to tell when the cupboard containing its food is being opened, or when its dish is being put on the floor. It will hear and respond to this from what can seem a remarkable distance away.

You may also find that your cat dislikes loud noise of any kind and that it will frequently leave a situation with this kind of disturbance. This is quite simply because its hearing is so much more sensitive than ours and it is receiving an unpleasant overload of noise.

Touch

As you may guess from the fact that your cat seems to enjoy being stroked, or rubbing itself around your legs, all of its body is very touch sensitive. Cats are sociable creatures, and enjoy physical contact.

Touch is also a very important means for them to find out about new things, and a cat will often experimentally pat an object it is not quite sure about, just to see what happens. Kittens do this very frequently, but the same behaviour can still be seen from time to time in adult cats.

3

VARIETIES OF CAT

CLASSIFICATION OF BREEDS

The original wild cats were all tabby in colour and their striped coats were ideally suited for camouflage purposes. After many years of careful selective breeding, there is now a whole range of different breeds in many attractive colours.

In the U.K. the classification of breeds is controlled by the Governing Council of the Cat Fancy (G.C.C.F), which publishes a list of the various breeds and their characteristics. I thank the G.C.C.F. for its assistance and permission to quote from its standards.

There are two classes of cat: long-haired and short-haired. The short-haired group is subdivided into British and Foreign varieties. The long-haired group is classified into the main British Standard (or Persian) type, and other individual Foreign varieties. Each breed is allocated its own number, for easy reference. Details such as the body markings, shape of head and body, colour of eyes, coat and type of tail are all included in the breed description. This usually includes any deviations from the accepted type which are termed 'faults'.

THE STANDARD FOR LONG-HAIRED CATS

Head: Large, round; wide face between tiny well-tufted ears; full cheeks; broad, short nose; large full eyes, bright, shiny and placed well apart.

Body: Short and stocky; a full tail with no bend or kink.

Limbs: Large and strong, but short and straight with plenty of bone. Feet should be neatly rounded.

Fig. 6.   Short-haired and long-haired cats.
Above: The foreign type Short-Hair.
Below The long-haired British (or Persian) type.

Coat: Full and flowing; hair longer on the neck and part way down the shoulders than on any other part of the body, giving the cat a 'frill'.

Faults: Large, pricked ears; long body with thin coat; thin tail; small, deep-set eyes; long nose; pinched muzzle; splay feet; bandy legs; convex spine.

THE STANDARD FOR SHORT-HAIRED CATS

BRITISH SHORT-HAIRS

Head: Round, good width of skull between tiny ears. Round, bright eyes, well-set; full cheeks; broad nose; unpinched muzzle.

Body: Stocky; short, broad, well-set tail without bend or kink, tapering slightly near the tip.

Limbs: Large, strong and well-boned, but not over-long. Small, well-rounded feet.

Coat: Dense and fine, but not wiry or woolly.

Faults: Large, pricked ears; small sunken eyes; long nose; pinched muzzle; spindly legs; splay feet; semi-long coat.

FOREIGN SHORT-HAIRS

Head: Long, wedge-shaped; wider at the eyes narrowing to a slim muzzle; large ears pricked wide at the base; almond-shaped eyes, slightly fuller in Abyssinians.

Body: Medium size, long and elegant.

Limbs: Thin and straight, slightly longer than those of the British Short-Hair; feet small and oval.

Tail: Thin and tapering to a point at the tip.

Coat: Short and dense.

Faults: Ears too upright and set either too straight on the head or too low, giving a wide appearance to the skull; short, thick tail; head too round; eyes too round, or too small and deep-set; nose too short; body too stocky; coat too long and not dense enough.

With the exception of the Manx and the curly-coated Rex cats, the above points are applicable to all the breeds.

LIST OF BREEDS

ABYSSINIAN

Fig. 7.   The Abyssinian.

There are various types of this short-haired cat, classified according to colour of coat. There should be no bars or other markings and the under parts of the cat's body should harmonise with the rest of the coat. The cat should not be too stocky and should have large green, amber or hazel eyes which are set well apart.

Russet Abyssinian *(breed no. 23)*

The Russet Abyssinian is the original type of Abyssinian and for this reason is sometimes also referred to as 'the Usual Abyssinian'. It has a reddish gold coat, with individual hairs which are ticked with black. The ticking may be double or treble. The pads on each foot should be black and the nose brick-red. The tail should be broad at the base, fairly long and tapering.

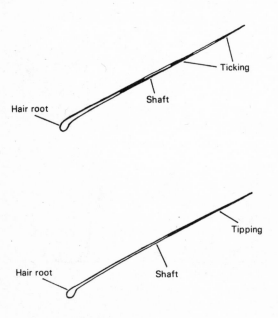

Fig. 8.   Ticking and tipping.
Above: The hair has a treble tick (e.g. the Abyssinian).
Below: The hair has a single tip (e.g. the Chinchilla).

Sorrel Abyssinian *(breed no. 23a)*

The Sorrel Abyssinian should have a lustrous copper-red coat ticked with chocolate, and the colour on the lower body parts should be dark apricot. The nose and pads are pink.

Chocolate Abyssinian *(breed no. 23b)*

The Chocolate Abyssinian should have a rich, coppery brown coat, ticked with dark chocolate. The base hair, abdomen and inside of the legs should be paler. The tip of the tail and solid colour on the hind legs should be dark chocolate. The nose should be pinkish chocolate and the pads should be chocolate.

Blue Abyssinian *(breed no. 23c)*

This variety has a blue-grey coat, ticked with a deeper steel-blue. The colour on the lower parts should be pale cream or oatmeal. The nose will be pink and the pads blue.

Lilac Abyssinian *(breed no. 23d)*

This cat should be a pinkish dove-grey with a 'powdered' effect, ticked with a deeper shade of the same colour. The base hair, abdomen and inside of the legs should be paler and the nose and pads should be mauvish pink.

Fawn Abyssinian *(breed no. 23e)*

This Abyssinian should be a warm fawn with a 'powdered' effect, ticked with a darker shade of the same colour. The under parts of the body should be paler, the nose should be pink and the pads mauvish pink.

Red Abyssinian *(breed no. 23f)*

The coat colour should be bright red, ticked with a deeper shade of the same colour. The base hair, abdomen and inside of the legs should be a slightly paler shade. The nose and pads should be pink.

Tortie Abyssinian

The Tortie (Tortoiseshell) Abyssinian exists in various coloured varieties and may also have a blaze of colour, or solid colour, on the legs and tail. The colours are:

Usual Tortie *(breed no. 23t)*	Mixture of golden brown and bright red, ticked in a deeper shade.
Sorrel Tortie *(breed no. 23at)*	Mixture of copper and bright red, ticked in a deeper shade.
Chocolate Tortie *(breed no. 23bt)*	Mixture of coppery brown and bright red, ticked in a deeper shade.
Blue Tortie *(breed no. 23ct)*	Mixture of blue-grey and rich cream with a 'powdered' effect, ticked with deeper shade. Nose and pads pink or mottled pink.
Lilac Tortie *(breed no. 23dt)*	Mixture of warm dove-grey and rich cream with 'powdered' effect, ticked with deeper shade. Nose and pads pink or mottled pink.
Fawn Tortie *(breed no. 23et)*	Mixture of warm fawn and rich cream with 'powdered' effect, ticked with deeper shade. Nose and pads pink or mottled pink.

Silver Abyssinian

In all Silver Abyssinian varieties the base coat should be white, and there should be no yellowish tinge to the fur. The following varieties can be found.

Black Silver *(breed no. 23s)*	Clear silver, ticked black; nose brick-red and pads black.
Sorrel Silver *(breed no. 23as)*	Silvery peach, ticked chocolate; nose and pads pink.

Chocolate Silver *(breed no. 23bs)*	Soft, silvery brown, ticked dark chocolate. Nose and pads pink or pinkish chocolate.
Blue Silver *(breed no. 23cs)*	Silvery blue-grey with a 'sparkling' effect, ticked deeper steel-blue. Nose dark pink and pads mauve.
Lilac Silver *(breed no. 23ds)*	Silver dove-grey with a 'sparkling' effect, ticked dove-grey. Nose and pads mauve.
Fawn Silver *(breed no. 23es)*	Silvery fawn with a 'sparkling' effect, ticked fawn. Nose and pads mauve.

ANGORA *(breed no. 62)*

The Angora should have a long, elegant body, fine legs and feet and a long, slender, plumed tail. It is a long-haired variety with a fine, silky coat and oriental-shaped eyes. The eye colour is usually green, except for Blue-Eyed and Odd-Eyed Whites. The ears may be tufted and the longer parts of the coat may wave slightly. The different varieties come in 'self' or single colours, tabbies, torties, smokes and shaded or spotted ranges.

Self-Coloured Angoras

Apart from the Whites, these cats should have coats of solid colour with no markings and no white hairs showing. Nose, eye rims and pads should be pink. The colours are:

Blue-Eyed White *(breed no. 62 14)*	
Odd-Eyed White *(breed no. 62 14b)*	Eyes one green and one blue.

Green-Eyed White
(breed no. 62 14c)

Black *(breed no. 62 15)*	Nose and eye rims black; pads black or brown.
Blue *(breed no. 62 16)*	Nose, eye rims and pads blue.
Chocolate *(breed no. 62 15b)*	Nose, eye rims and pads brown.
Lilac *(breed no. 62 15c)*	Nose, eye rims and pads pinkish lilac.
Red Self *(breed no. 62 15d)*	Nose, eye rims and pads pink. Slight freckling in coat permissible.
Cream *(breed no. 62 15f)*	Nose, eye rims and pads pink, some freckling permissible.
Cinnamon *(breed no. 62 15k)*	Nose and eye rims cinnamon and pads pinkish brown.
Caramel *(breed no. 62 15n)*	Nose, eye rims and pads brownish blue.
Fawn *(breed no. 62 15r)*	Nose, eye rims and pads pinkish fawn. Coat warm mushroom, not bluish.

Tortie Angoras *(breed no. 62 21)*
The Tortoiseshell Angoras should not have any tabby markings in their base coat. Instead, they must have patches of colour in red, cream or beige which may show some tabby patterning. A blaze is permissible. The nose, eye rims and pads may be either pink or matched in line with the coat colour.

Smoke Angoras *(breed no. 62 36)*
The base coat should be silvery-white, and between one third and two thirds of the total hair length. The smoking can be in any of the accepted Angora colours and the head and face should match the body as closely as possible. Too much silver brindling is undesirable, as is too much tabby marking although some faint marking is allowed.

Shaded Angoras *(breed no. 62 43)*
The coat in both the Standard and the Silver-Shaded Angoras can be shaded (or tipped) in any of the accepted colours. The body shading should be as free from tabby markings as possible, although there should be tabby patterning on the head. There should be a denser concentration of colour along the spine and tail, getting lighter over the flanks and becoming much paler on the under parts of the body.

Tabby Angoras *(breed nos. 62 18, 62 19 and 62 20)*
The tabby pattern in both Standard and Silver Tabbies can be Classic Tabby, Spotted Tabby, Mackerel Tabby or Ticked Tabby. The pattern in all cases should be well-defined, although the long coat can at times obscure this and will need to be smoothed down.

ASIAN *(breed no. 72)*
The Asian cats are elegant in appearance, following the Foreign type of either Short- or Long-Hair varieties. It is really a classification for cats of the Burmese type, but not having Burmese colouring and coat. The eyes should be any shade in the yellow to green range, although green is preferred for the silver varieties. The eyes should be wide-set and neither almond-shaped nor round.

The body should be medium-sized and well-muscled, and the legs should be of medium length with the front legs slightly shorter than the back ones. The paws should be oval and the colour of the pads, nose and eye rims should correspond with the coat colour. The tail should be medium to long, finishing with a rounded tip. The female Asians are noticeably smaller and daintier than the males.

The breeds within the Asian group are:

Burmilla   The Shaded or Tipped variety

Asian Smoke   The Smoke variety

Asian Tabbies   The Ticked, Spotted, Mackerel or Classic Tabby varieties

Bombay   The Self-Black variety

Tiffanie   The Long-Haired variety.

Apart from the Bombay which is black only, all the Asians are found in the following colours: black, blue, chocolate, lilac, red, caramel, apricot, black tortie, cream, blue tortie, chocolate tortie, lilac tortie, caramel tortie or a silver version of any of these.

BALINESE *(breed no. 61)*
The Balinese is a long-haired variety of Siamese and follows its general shape and colouring. The ears may be tufted and the tail should be long and plume-like. The coat should be fine and silky in texture and definitely not woolly. The colours are seal, blue, chocolate, lilac, red, cream, tortie and tabby in all shades.

BI-COLOURED *(breed nos. 12a Long-Hair and 31 Short-Hair)*
Bi-coloured cats have coats of any colour mixed with white,

but the patches of colour should be clear, even and well-distributed. Not more than two thirds of the cat's coat should be coloured and the face should have coloured and white patches. The eyes should be large and round, of a deep orange or copper colour.

BIRMAN *(breed no. 13c)*
This is a long-haired cat with colouring similar to the Siamese, except that it has white feet. The colour may be Blue Point or Seal Point. The Seal Point Birman has a dark brown face, tail and legs with a pale beige body. The Blue Point variety has a blue-grey face, tail and legs and a bluish white body. The eyes are bright blue.

BLACK LONG-HAIR *(breed no. 1)*
The Black Long-Hair, or 'Black Persian', should have the typical long, flowing Persian coat, but in a lustrous raven black colour, with no other colours or shadings present. The eyes should be copper or orange with no green in them.

BLACK SHORT-HAIR *(breed no. 15)*
The Black Short-Hair should conform to the normal rules set for British Short-Hairs, and in addition should follow the colouring pattern of the Black Long-Hair. There should be no tinge of rust in the coat and the eyes should be copper or orange with no hint of green.

BLUE LONG-HAIR *(breed no. 3)*
The coat of a Blue Long-Hair can be any shade of blue including lavender, but it must be a good even colour without any marking or shading and must have no white hairs. Eyes must be deep burnished copper, almost red in tone, with no green in them.

BRITISH BLUE SHORT-HAIR *(breed no. 16)*

The coat colour should be light or medium unshaded blue and the eyes should be copper or orange, the deeper the shade the better. The nose should be blue, as should the pads.

Fig. 9.   The British Blue.

BLUE CREAM LONG-HAIR *(breed no. 13)*

In the Blue Cream the coat should not have patches of colour; the blue and the cream hairs should be intermingled, so that the whole effect is of a single colour 'like shot silk'. The eyes must be deep copper or orange and the coat should be very silky and dense. The Blue Cream Long-Hair is produced by mating a Blue with a Cream, but a side-effect of this is that unfortunately most Blue Cream males are sterile.

BLUE CREAM SHORT-HAIR *(breed no. 28)*
As in the Long-Hair breed, the blue and cream hairs must intermingle softly. The eyes should be orange or copper and the nose blue, and the pads should be either blue or pink.

BRITISH TIPPED *(breed no. 39)*
This cat is a short-haired variety and must conform to the standard for British Short-Hair breeds. The colours may be any colour accepted in recognised British breeds with the addition of brown, chocolate and lilac. The undercoat should be as white as possible with coloured tipping evenly distributed. Black tipped cats have green eyes, but all other colours have orange or copper eye colour.

BURMESE
Burmese are dainty short-haired cats. Their heads do have a distinct wedge-shape, but they are a little shorter than those of the Siamese. Their eyes should be almond in shape, slanting to the nose, preferably in a golden yellow shade. Green eyes are considered a bad fault in a Burmese.

The coat should be close-lying and glossy. In the Brown Burmese the colour must be a rich, dark brown, shading down to a lighter colour on the abdomen. There should be no markings or white hairs. The ears should be quite wide at the base and in profile show a slight forward tilt.

The Blue Burmese are exactly the same in type, but the body colour should be of slate or bluish grey with a silver sheen. The colour on the back should be darker than that on the abdomen.

In both types, the kittens are lighter in colour but darken as they reach maturity. Although they appear dainty, Burmese should be well-muscled and their legs should be slim with neatly rounded feet.

Burmese are divided into the following breeds according to colour:

Brown Burmese *(breed no. 27)*
Coat colour rich seal-brown with slightly darker ears and face.

Blue Burmese *(breed no. 27a)*
Coat soft silver-grey, very slightly darker on the back and tail.

Chocolate Burmese *(breed no. 27b)*
Coat colour warm milk chocolate with slightly darker ears and face.

Lilac Burmese *(breed no. 27c)*
Pale delicate dove-grey.

Red Burmese *(breed no. 27d)*
Coat colour light tangerine. Ears should be darker than the back.

Brown Tortie Burmese *(breed no. 27e)*
Brown coat colour with some red hairs and no bars or obvious markings.

Cream Burmese *(breed no. 27f)*
Coat colour rich cream.

Blue Tortie Burmese *(breed no. 27g)*
Coat colour blue and cream colouring. No obvious marks or bars.

Chocolate Tortie Burmese *(breed no. 27h)*
Coat colour chocolate and red colouring. No obvious marks or bars.

Lilac Tortie Burmese *(breed no. 27j)*
Coat colour lilac and cream, without any marks or bars.

CHINCHILLA *(breed no. 10)*
The Chinchilla belongs to the Long-Hair group of cats and has the most beautiful coat. The undercoat is pure white and the hairs on the head, back, flanks, ears and tail are tipped with

black. The tipping must be very evenly distributed and the legs, feet and stomach must be pure white. The top of the nose must be brick-red and the visible skin of the eyelids and pads of the feet should be black. The eyes should be large and round, coloured emerald-green or blue.

Fig. 10. The Chinchilla.

CHOCOLATE LONG-HAIR *(breed no. 50b)*
This cat has a medium to dark chocolate-brown coat, free from marking or shading or white hairs. The fur should be long, thick and soft in texture. The eyes are rounded and deep orange or copper.

COLOUR POINT LONG-HAIR *(breed no. 13b)*
The Colour Point is a true Long-Hair in type, but it follows the

Siamese in colouring. The eyes should always be large, round and pale. The colours accepted are these:

1. *Seal Point* with cream body colour
2. *Blue Point* with glacial-white body colour
3. *Chocolate Point* with ivory body colour
4. *Lilac Point* with magnolia body colour
5. *Red Point* with off-white body colour
6. *Tortie Point* with cream body colour
7. *Cream*
8. *Blue Cream*
9. *Chocolate Cream*
10. *Lilac Cream*
11. *Tabby*

CREAM LONG-HAIR *(breed no. 5)*
The colour of the ideal Cream should be a lovely pale shade of true cream, sound to the roots. There should be no shading or marking, especially no red tinge, as this is considered a major fault. The eyes should be a deep copper colour.

CREAM SHORT-HAIR *(breed no. 17)*
The shades of lighter cream are preferred in this breed, and there should be no white hairs showing. There should be no shading or markings and the eyes should be copper or orange.

CREAM CAMEO *(breed no. 52)*
This is a long-haired cat with a white undercoat shading to tips of cream or blue cream. The deepest colour should be shown on the 'points' (i.e. the head, feet and legs), while the lighter colour should be on the neck frill, sides and abdomen. The eyes should be deep orange or copper in colour.

Within this breed the following colours appear:

1. *Shell*
2. *Shaded*

3. *Cream Smoke*
4. *Blue Cream*

EXOTIC SHORT-HAIRS *(breed no. 70)*

The general standard for Exotic Short-Hairs is a large, round head with a good breadth of skull and small, round-tipped ears set wide apart. The nose should be short and broad and the chin must be strong above a short, thick neck. Eyes should be large and round.

The body must be stocky and the cat as a whole should be quite large and well-muscled. The legs must be short and sturdy and the paws should be large and round. The tail will be relatively short, and the coat will be dense and plush, standing out from the body. Major faults are considered to be orange in the eyes of green-eyed cats, or vice versa.

Blue-Eyed White Exotic *(breed no. 70 14)*
Pure white; deep blue eyes; pink nose and pads.

Orange-Eyed White Exotic *(breed no. 70 14a)*
Pure white; deep orange eyes; pink nose and pads.

Odd-Eyed White Exotic *(breed no. 70 14b)*
Pure white; pink nose and pads; one eye blue and one orange.

Black Exotic *(breed no. 70 15)*
Lustrous black, no rust colour or white hairs; nose, eye rims and pads black; eyes deep orange.

Chocolate Exotic *(breed no. 70 15b)*
Medium to dark chocolate, including nose, eye rims and pads; deep orange eyes.

Lilac Exotic *(breed no. 70 15c)*
Lilac, including nose, eye rims and pads; eyes deep orange.

Red Self Exotic
(breed no. 70 15d)

Deep red; may have ghost tail rings; nose, eye rims and pads deep pink; eyes deep orange.

Blue Exotic
(breed no. 70 16)

Medium to pale blue; nose, eye rims and pads blue-grey; eyes deep orange.

Cream Exotic
(breed no. 70 17)

Pale to medium cream; nose, eye rims and pads pink; ghost tail rings may be visible; eyes deep orange.

Tabby Exotics
The Tabby Exotics are found in Classic, Mackerel and Spotted Tabby varieties in the following colours: silver, red, brown, blue, chocolate, lilac, cream and tortie.

Bi-Colour and Tri-Colour Exotics *(breed nos. 70 31 and 70 22)*
These cats should have white coats patched with the appropriate colours. No more than one half of the cat's body should be white, and no more than two thirds should be coloured. There should be no white hairs present in the coloured patches. The face must have patches of colour and white, and the tail should be fully coloured. Eyes should be orange, copper or deep gold.

Smoke Exotic *(breed no. 70 36)*
The Smoke can be found in any of the recognised colours, with the white base coat contrasting strongly with the dark colour-shading in the back, head and feet.

Tipped Exotic *(breed no. 70 39)*
The tipping is acceptable in any of the recognised Long-Hair colours and the base coat should be as white as possible. Tipping

should be present on the back, head and tail, giving a 'sparkling' appearance. It can extend to the legs, but the under parts of the body should be pure white. Cats with black tipping should have blue-green or emerald-green eyes, black or brown pads and brick-red noses; all others should have copper, orange or deep gold eyes, and pads and noses corresponding with coat colour.

Colour-Pointed Exotics *(breed no. 70 40)*
In these cats there should be a good contrast between the 'points' (mask, legs, feet and tail) and the body colour. Eye colour should be pure blue. Nose, eye rims and pads should tone with the points' colour. Varieties found are: seal, blue, chocolate, lilac, red, cream, tortie and tabby.

Pewter Exotic *(breed no. 70 73)*
This cat must be white, evenly shaded with black to give the overall pewter colour. The base coat should be pure white. The eyes are copper, orange or deep gold and the nose is brick-red outlined with black. Pads should be black or dark brown.

Blue-Pewter Exotic *(breed no. 70 73a)*
The colouring is as for the Pewter Exotic except that it is shaded with blue and the nose and pads are also blue.

Golden Exotic *(breed no. 70 74)*
The base coat is apricot, deepening to gold. The eye rims and nose are outlined with brown or black, and the pads are the same colour. The back, flanks, head and tail are gold, tipped with black or brown; this is a much heavier tipping effect than in the Tipped Exotic. Eyes must be green or blue-green.

Shaded Silver Exotic and Shaded Blue Silver Exotic
(breed nos. 70 75 and 70 75a)
Both of these varieties must have a pure white base coat and tipping on the head, back, legs and flanks in black or blue for the blue silver type. The tipping must be one third of the total

hair length. The eye rims, lips and nose must be outlined in the same shade as the tipping, and the pads should correspond in colour. The Shaded Silver Exotic has a brick-red nose and green or blue-green eyes; the Shaded Blue Silver variety has a blue nose and orange or deep gold eyes.

ORIENTAL SHORT-HAIRS

FOREIGN WHITE *(breed no. 35)*
This is a short-haired cat with a pure white coat and vivid blue eyes. The coat must be purest white, short and silky. The nose and the insides of the ears must be pink and the eyes must be brilliant blue. They are long, slender cats with the rump carried a little higher than the shoulders. The cat should have a well-rounded and elegant look.

FOREIGN BLACK *(breed no. 37)*
This should be a graceful cat with short hair, green oriental eyes and a jet-black coat. It must be well-balanced with fine legs and a wedge-shaped head. The nose and eye rims should be black and the pads brown or black.

FOREIGN BLUE *(breed no. 37a)*
As for Foreign Black, but light to medium blue coat. Blue nose, eye rims and pads.

FOREIGN CARAMEL *(breed no. 37n)*
As for the Black, but bluish fawn coat, nose, eye rims and pads.

FOREIGN CINNAMON *(breed no. 37k)*
As for the Black, but warm cinnamon brown coat, eye rims and nose; pads cinnamon or pink.

FOREIGN CREAM *(breed no. 37f)*
As for the Black, but eyes can be all shades from copper to green, and the coat should be a cool-toned cream. There may be a slight freckling in the coat, and the nose, eye rims and pads should be pink.

FOREIGN FAWN *(breed no. 37r)*
As for the Black, but the coat is warm mushroom, with a definite pink tinge. A cold or blue shade is considered to be a fault. The nose, eye rims and pads should be a pinkish fawn.

FOREIGN LILAC *(breed no. 29c)*
Like the Black, but the coat is frosty grey with a distinct pinkish tone. It has a similar appearance to a Havana cat, except for the colouring.

FOREIGN RED *(breed no. 37d)*
Similar to the other Orientals, but with a rich red coat. There may be some tabby markings or freckling present, but there should be no white hairs. The nose, eye rims and pads are pink.

HAVANA *(breed no. 29)*
The Havana is of the same Oriental type, with a rich chestnut brown coat and green, almond-shaped eyes. The hair is close-lying and glossy, and the nose and whiskers are the same colour as the coat. There should be no markings on the body, or points of deeper colouration. There must be no kink in the tail and the pads of the feet should be a pinkish shade.

OTHER ORIENTALS OR FOREIGN CATS
The Orientals may also be found in Tabby, Tipped, Smoke and Shaded varieties.

KORAT *(breed no. 34)*
This is a Foreign Short-Hair with a heart-shaped head and large,

prominent eyes. The eye colour is normally green, but amber is acceptable too. The coat is silvery-blue, tipped with silver.

LILAC LONG-HAIR *(breed no. 50c)*
This breed should have a pinkish, dove-grey coat, evenly coloured all over. The eyes should be orange or copper.

MAINE COON *(breed no. 64)*
The Maine Coon is a muscular, hardy-looking cat with a thick long-haired coat and a substantial appearance, largely due to its size and shaggy coat. It should have a solid, square look to its body and a long bushy tail. The coat is waterproof, achieved by a glossy topcoat and a thick undercoat. Both the ears and feet may be tufted. The ears are large and tall, and the eyes are round in a green, gold or copper shade. Colours may be white, black, blue, red, cream, bi-colour, tortie, tabby, smoke or shaded.

MANX *(breed no. 25)*
The Manx cat and how it became tail-less is one of the mysteries of the feline race. In a perfect specimen of Manx cat, there should be a distinct V-shaped nick in which you can lay your finger at the base of the spine (this is where the tail starts in other cats). The rump should be rounded and the hind legs should be considerably longer than the front ones.

Manx cats can be any colour. The coat should be short and of good texture, showing a 'double coat' with a longer outer coat and a shorter one underneath. There must be a good depth of flank.

The eyes can be any colour and the head should be larger than that of the British Short-Hair, with a longer nose. The cheeks should be prominent and the ears should be wide at the base, tapering to a slight point.

NORWEGIAN FOREST CAT *(breed no. 67)*
The Norwegian Forest Cat is a Long-Hair, with a triangular head and a strong chin. The ears are tufted and set high on the head.

Fig. 11. The Manx.

Eyes are large and may be any colour, regardless of coat shade.
It is a powerfully-built cat with a long body and slightly longer
hind legs than front ones. Its tail is long and bushy, and like the
Maine Coon it has a water-repellent top coat over a woolly base
coat. All varieties and shadings may be found except for lilac,
chocolate and the Siamese patterns.

PEWTER LONG-HAIR *(breed no. 53)*
This cat has a white coat shaded with black to give a 'pewter'
effect. It should have orange eyes, and follow the standard for
Long-Hairs.

RAGDOLL *(breed no. 66)*

This cat is floppy when handled, which is why it was called Ragdoll. Breeders claim that it is especially tolerant of being handled by children. It is a Long-Hair with a silky, dense coat and there should be a good contrast in colour between the points and the base coat. Lack of contrast is a fault. Generally it is a medium-sized cat with a long, muscular body, finishing in a bushy tail which is quite long and tapers towards the tip. The ears are medium-sized and tip forward slightly. The eye colour is blue, deep blue being preferred, and the eyes should be large, oval and slanting. The legs are fairly strong and the paws are large, round and tufted.

Ragdoll varieties are as follows:

Seal Point   Even beige, lightening to cream; points deep seal-brown.

Blue Point   Bluish white; points greyish blue.

Chocolate Point   Ivory; points milk chocolate.

Lilac Point   Magnolia white; points pinkish grey.

Colour-Pointed   No white anywhere; points contrasting well with base colour.

Mitted Ragdoll   White blaze on nose; under parts, chin and chest white; the front paws have white mittens; the hind legs white boots; points should contrast well, and nose and pads should match points.

Bi-Colour Ragdoll   Mask should have an inverted 'V' of white on the forehead extending down over the nose and chin. The chest and under parts should be white, as should the front legs. The back legs should be white only to the hock. A small amount of white can be present on the rest of the body, but not on the points which should be well-defined in the appropriate colour. Nose and pads will be pink.

RED CAMEO *(breed no. 51)*

This long-haired cat has beautiful contrasting colours in its coat. The under parts of the coat must be white and the tipping red or tortoiseshell, with deep-coloured points. Included in this group are the colours:

1. *Shell*

2. *Shaded*

3. *Red Smoke*

4. *Tortie Cameo*

RED-SELF *(breed no. 4)*

It is very difficult to produce a perfect specimen of this long-haired breed, since the coat must be a deep, rich, clear red and free of any markings. Generally cats of this breed show some tabby markings on the coat. The eyes should be large and deep copper in colour.

REX CATS

These are short-haired cats, originating from Devon and Cornwall. Their coats are curly, sometimes with unfortunate bare patches because of the way the coat curls. This is considered a fault; both Cornish and Devon Rexes should ideally be well-covered by their coat. In both varieties the whiskers can be curly or very short. The coat must be short, full and noticeably wavy.

Fig. 12.   The Devon Rex.

Cornish Rex *(breed no. 33)*
The Cornish Rex is larger than the Devon Rex and more like a
Foreign Short-Hair in appearance. The head and body are long
in shape, and the coat is denser and less tightly-curled than that
of the Devon Rex. White markings are accepted on the coat, but
these should be symmetrical (except in the Tortie and White).

Devon Rex *(breed no. 33a)*
The Devon Rex has enormous ears and can have a coat of any
colour except the bi-colours. Any white marking other than tortie
and white is considered a fault.

RUSSIAN BLUE (breed no. 16a)

This is classified under the Foreign Short-Hair section, and differs in every way from the British Blue except in colour. The body of the Russian Blue is long and slender, with a long, wedge-shaped head. The ears are large, pointed and wide at the base. It has long, slim legs and almond-shaped eyes of a deep grass-green colour. The coat should be a clear, even blue throughout, free of any tabby markings. The overall impression should be of a long, graceful cat. Russian Blues are generally quiet cats, not using their voices often. There are also White and Black Russian varieties.

SIAMESE (breed nos. 24 and 32)

The Siamese is the most popular of all breeds, and all varieties follow the same basic type, but with colour variations. They follow the standard for Foreign Short-Hairs and should be beautifully balanced with a long, lithe body, fine legs and a long and tapering tail. The ears should be large and pricked, with a wide base.

In all colour variations the face (or 'mask'), ears, legs, feet and tail (i.e. the 'points') must show dense and well-defined colour. All the points should match in the depth of colour, with a clear contrast between these and the overall body colour. Shading can appear on the back and flanks, but the bib, chest and abdomen should be pale.

Siamese are classified into the following varieties:

Seal Point (breed no. 24)	Cream body coat; points seal-brown.
Blue Point (breed no. 24a)	Glacial-white body coat; points light blue.
Chocolate Point (breed no. 24b)	Ivory body coat; points milk chocolate.

Fig. 13.   The Siamese.
Note the dark area of face, called 'The Mask'.

Lilac Point   Magnolia body coat; points
(breed no. 24c)   pinkish-grey.

Tabby Point
(breed no. 32)

Pale coat; striped tabby marking; varieties are seal, blue, chocolate, lilac, red, cream.

Red Point
(breed no. 32a)

White/apricot shading; points reddish gold.

Seal Tortie Point
(breed no. 32b (1))

Fawn body; seal-brown/red points.

Blue Tortie Point
(breed no. 32b (2))

White; shading blue and cream; points blue/cream.

Chocolate Tortie Point
(breed no. 32b (3))

Ivory; shading chocolate; points chocolate/red and apricot.

Lilac Tortie Point
(breed no. 32b (4))

Off-white; shading lilac; points cream and lilac/cream.

Cream Point
(breed no. 32c)

White; shading cream; pale points.

In a Seal Point the colour must be even, pale fawn shading gradually to cream on the abdomen and chest. Mask, legs, ears, tail and feet must be a dense and clearly-defined seal-brown. Eyes must be clear, bright and decidedly blue, almond-shaped and slanting towards the nose.

The Blue Point follows the same standard, but the body colour should be glacial-white, shading gradually into blue on the back (the same cold tone as the points but of a lighter shade). The eyes of this variety should be a clear, bright china-blue.

Siamese make devoted pets, but they are far from quiet,

especially when in season. They are also noted for their powers of destruction, particularly using their claws on soft furnishings. Strict training is required from an early age to prevent this.

If left unneutered they will produce numerous offspring, the litters varying from three to eight each time. Kittens are born pure white and the points become visible at about two or three weeks old, darkening gradually from then on. In the early days of the Siamese, a kink in the tail was normal, but now it is considered a fault, with straight tails being preferred.

SMOKE LONG-HAIR *(breed no. 6)*

The Smoke 'Persian' is a very handsome cat. Its coat is light silver, almost 'off-white' underneath and tipped with dense black on the back and sides. The neck frill, flanks and ear tips are pale and silvery, which make a striking contrast with the black-tipped fur, and the jet-black face, head and paws. The colour should be even and not smudgy. The cat should be large and stocky, with short legs. The eyes are deep copper or orange.

BLUE SMOKE LONG-HAIR *(breed no. 6a)*

The Blue Smoke is similar in all respects to the Smoke except that the points and tipping of the fur are blue instead of black.

SMOKES (SHORT-HAIRS) *(breed no. 36)*

This short-haired variety has a pale silver undercoat with black on the points and tipping. The eyes can be yellow or orange.

SOMALI *(breed no. 63)*

The Somali follows the Foreign type Long-Hair standard, and occurs in the same range of colours as the Abyssinian cat. It is sometimes referred to as the Usual Somali. There is also a short-haired variety, known as the Somali Variant. It is a lithe, active cat with good muscular development and a fine, soft coat. There should be at least three bands of ticking on the hairs, although this may not be fully developed until the cat is a mature adult.

The eyes are almond-shaped and set well apart, with dark lid skin and encircled by light-coloured 'spectacles'. Above each eye there is a short dark vertical 'pencil' line, with a similar line running from the upper lid towards the ear.

SPOTTED (SHORT-HAIR) *(breed no. 30)*
The Spotted cats follow the tabby pattern of colouration with the addition of blue and cream, but except for the head there must be no stripes, unlike other tabbies. Spots of colour can be round, oval or rosette-shaped, but must be distinct and entirely separate from each other. In all other respects these cats follow the standard for the British Short-Hair.

Note so-called mayoral rings on chest

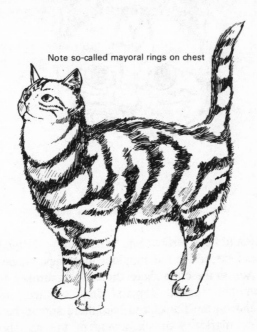

Fig. 14. The Tabby.

THE TABBIES

The Tabbies are sub-divided into three groups: the Brown, the Red and the Silver. All can be found in both Long-Hair and Short-Hair varieties, the colouring being the same for both coats.

All markings should be clearly defined and the coat should be dense. The forehead should be covered with delicate lines of colour, running down the face and converging on the base of the nose. This will often form a classic 'M' shape, a bit like frown lines.

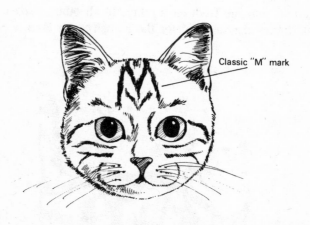

Classic "M" mark

Fig. 15. Facial markings on a Tabby.

There should be a vertical line which runs over the back of the head and extends to the shoulder markings, shaped like a butterfly. Across the chest there should be unbroken bands of colour, sometimes called 'mayoral rings' or 'necklaces' (see Fig. 14), and on the flanks and legs there should be regular stripes. The markings on each side of the cat should be identical. The tail should be evenly banded from the base to the tip. All tabby cats should also be spotted with colour in the abdominal region.

The cats will follow the recognised standards for either long- or short-haired cats, with additional standards for markings and colour. They are grouped as follows:

LONG-HAIR

Silver Tabby *(breed no. 7)*

Brown Tabby *(breed no. 8)*

Red Tabby *(breed no. 9)*

SHORT-HAIR

Silver Tabby *(breed no. 18)*

Red Tabby *(breed no. 19)*

Brown Tabby *(breed no. 20)*

Oriental Spotted Tabby *(breed no. 38)*

The Brown Tabbies should have a coat which is rich tawny-sable, with the tabby markings in black. The eyes are hazel or copper in colour. Red Tabbies have a deep, rich, red coat, with the tabby markings shown in a deeper shade of red. The eyes must be a deep copper. Silver Tabbies have a pure pale silver coat, with black tabby markings. The eyes should be green or hazel.

In the Tabby varieties the chief 'faults' are considered to be light-coloured chins; light tips of tails; poorly-defined markings and back markings which are too solid in appearance.

The Mackerel Tabby pattern of marking has the same head marking as the Classic Tabby described previously. In addition, a narrow unbroken line runs from the back of the head to the base of the tail. The rest of the body is covered with unbroken narrow lines running vertically down from the spine line.

Oriental Spotted Tabbies

These cats must be oriental in type, with a long, elegant body, fine legs and a wedge-shaped head. Good clear spotting is essential, with clear rings on the tail. Several colours are accepted and classified:

Brown (breed no. 38)

Blue (breed no. 38a)

Chocolate (breed no. 38b)

Lilac (breed no. 38c)

Red (breed no. 38d)

Cream (breed no. 38e)

TONKINESE *(breed no. 74)*

The Tonkinese is a short-haired cat which can be placed between the Burmese and Siamese breeds, from which it descended. It is generally a relaxed, friendly cat, well-proportioned with a firm, muscular body and slim legs. The Tonkinese coat is fine and short, with a silky sheen to it.

The eyes are more open than almond, but not truly round. Eye colour must be greenish blue to pale blue, but not bright blue. The points should be much darker than the rest of the coat, merging gently into it rather than forming a sharp contrast. Colour varieties are:

Brown	Light brown; darker seal points.
Blue	Blue silver-grey; darker slate-grey points.
Chocolate	Milk chocolate; darker chocolate points.

Fig. 16. The Oriental Spotted Tabby.

Lilac	Pale pinkish dove-grey; darker points.
Red	Light red; darker points.

Cream	Warm cream; darker points.
Brown Tortie	Seal-brown, patched with red; darker points.
Blue Tortie	Bluish silver-grey, patched with cream; darker points.
Chocolate Tortie	Milk chocolate, patched with red; darker points.
Lilac Tortie	Pale pinkish dove-grey, patched with cream; darker points.
Brown Tabby	Light brown with darker tabby markings; all colours darker on points.
Blue Tabby	Blue silver-grey with darker tabby markings; all colours darker on points.
Chocolate Tabby	Milk chocolate; darker tabby markings; all colours darker on points.
Lilac Tabby	Pale pinkish dove-grey; darker tabby markings; all colours darker on points.
Red Tabby	Light red; darker tabby markings; all colours darker on points.
Cream Tabby	Warm cream; hotter cream tabby markings; denser colour on points.
Tortie Tabbies	Follow the Tortie colours but can be mottled.

TORTOISESHELLS *(breed nos. 11 (Long-Hair) and 21 (Short-Hair))*

These cats are nearly always female, being used frequently for breeding purposes. One queen can produce many different colours from one mating (e.g. creams, blue creams, reds, blacks, whites and blues).

The markings of a Tortie should be in three colours: black, red and cream. They should be as bright as possible, and mixed in such a way that the cat's coat has a 'patched' appearance. In the Tortie, intermingling or blending of colour is considered a fault. The patches of different colour should cover the body and legs.

Blaze Facial Marking

A cream or red blaze is desirable and the eyes should be brilliant copper or orange. The Long-Hair and Short-Hair varieties will each conform to the appropriate breed standard.

Ears may be dark coloured

White blaze

Fig. 17. Blaze Facial Marking.

TORTOISESHELL AND WHITE
(breed nos. 12 (Long-Hair) and 22 (Short-Hair))
The difference between this variety and the Tortoiseshell is the
addition of white to the three original colours. White should

Fig. 18.   Long-Hair Tortoiseshell and White.

appear on the chest, feet and legs, as well as the blaze, but there should be no white hairs mingling in with the other colours. Like the other Tortoiseshells, they are nearly always female, with the rare males being sterile. The eye colour should be copper or orange.

TURKISH VAN CATS *(breed no. 13d)*

Turkish cats are fonder of water than other breeds, and so are sometimes called the 'swimming cats'. They are neither true Long-Hairs nor true Short-Hairs; their coat is somewhere in between the two. They look more foreign than British in type, with a short wedge-shaped head and large upright ears. Their noses are longish, and they are quite sturdy and muscular in build.

Their colouring is pure white with auburn markings on the face, body and tail, while the nose, pads and the inside of the ears are a delicate pink. Their eyes are round and a light amber in colour.

WHITE LONG-HAIRS

There are three varieties of this breed, depending on eye colour. These are:

Blue-Eyed *(breed no. 2)*

Orange-Eyed *(breed no. 2a)*

Odd-Eyed *(breed no. 2b)*

The Whites have a long, soft, flowing coat, without any marks or shading, and particularly no yellow tinge. The Blue-Eyed Whites have a tendency to deafness, but this is not shared by those with orange or odd eyes (one blue and one orange).

WHITE SHORT-HAIR (BLUE-EYED) *(breed no. 14)*
This cat follows the standard for Short-Hairs and has the same body and eye colouring as the Blue-Eyed White Long-Hair.

CAT SHOWS AND CAT CLUBS
The G.C.C.F. sets the regulations controlling cat shows and all pedigree cats shown must be registered with them. They also publish a guide called 'Showing Cats' which is useful for a beginner. In addition, there are numerous local cat clubs and it is a good idea for a novice to join one of these. (A list of them can be obtained from the G.C.C.F.) In this way you can be sure of some help and support at your first show.

Many cat clubs are regionally based and may organise a social programme as well. Also, they will often publish a newsletter giving details of the various shows and how to enter them. Generally there will be a registration form and an appropriate fee for each show.

Conditions of Showing
Show cats are judged on their overall appearance and how they behave at the show, as well as how well they conform to the standard laid down for their particular breed. Non-pedigree cats may also be shown and there are usually special classes for these.

It is quite normal for a vet to examine all cats at the beginning of a show, to ensure that they are in good health. A cat is also only allowed to be shown once within a fourteen day period, to minimise any stress caused to it. In addition to being fit and healthy, cats must also be well-groomed and have perfectly clean and sound claws and teeth.

They also have to be willing to be handled by complete strangers and to accept being kept in a pen next to a lot of other cats without making a fuss about it. General procedure at a show is for the cats to be kept in pens lined with a white blanket, containing water and food bowls and a litter tray. They are not usually fed before showing, but owners should provide food for them after judging has taken place.

Judging
All owners must leave the room before the judges and stewards make their rounds. They will take the cats out and examine them one by one. Obviously a cat which struggles, or miaows in protest during this examination, is not going to make as good an impression as one which accepts it quite happily. A calm temperament is therefore very important in show cats.

The winning cats will be awarded rosettes and a small prize. (Financial rewards are not particularly large in this sort of show; most owners do it for fun and the prestige of winning something occasionally.) Cat shows are sociable occasions, though, and it can be very interesting to meet other people with a similar hobby and to see their cats.

Exemption and Championship Shows
As a novice, it is better to begin with an 'exemption show' rather than a 'championship show' because the competition will be less fierce. Exemption shows are generally held between April and September, when long-haired cats are moulting, stud toms are in the mating season and so may not be so even-tempered, and many queens will be having litters. The main championship shows are held from September to March.

Only unneutered cats may enter a championship class; neutered animals have their own 'premier' class. Kittens under nine months old may only enter the special 'kitten' classes. To achieve the honour of 'Champion' or 'Premier', the cat must win three classes under three different judges at different cat shows. It may then be entered for the 'champion of champions' class, and if it wins this three times it can then be called a 'Grand Champion'.

4

ACQUIRING A CAT

Cats are extremely appealing creatures, but before you rush out to get one, do consider what sort of commitment you are making. A cat will be with you for a good many years, more than a decade in most cases, and will require some attention every day of its life. At the very least this will include daily feeding.

You will have to pay annual vet's fees for vaccinations, cover the cost of neutering if necessary, plus pay for care in the event of any illness. If you go away on holiday, then you will have to pay fees to a boarding cattery. The cost of all this can be multiplied by the number of cats you choose to have.

Also bear in mind that a new cat or kitten will need a lot of attention while it is growing up and learning about the world and you. Having said that, becoming a cat owner can be a delightful and extremely rewarding experience, provided that you start with the right attitude.

OBTAINING A CAT OR KITTEN

There are a number of decisions which you need to make, once you have decided to become a cat owner. The first is whether to have an adult cat or a kitten. To some extent this may depend on what you are offered; some people become owners because they have a friend who needs a good home for a cat or kittens which he or she is unable to care for. If you are in this situation, then the decision is already made for you. Otherwise you will need to think carefully about it.

A kitten will initially be more demanding of its new owner

than an adult cat, because it is young and needs constant stimulation while it is learning and growing. However, it will also be that much more adaptable because it is not set in its ways, and you will probably not have to contend with any habits it has picked up from its previous home or homes. In general, a kitten will settle into a new environment faster than a mature animal will.

There is a definite advantage to having a kitten rather than a cat if you have a dog already, or if you have children. Children will adore playing with a kitten, and it will be far more likely to adapt to sharing a house with a dog than a mature cat which has spent much of its life treating dogs as mortal enemies.

The owner's age is also a matter for consideration. It is clearly not kind or sensible to obtain a young kitten for an aging grandparent, because the kitten will not only exhaust their patience, it will probably also outlive them. An adult cat would be preferable in these circumstances, being older, calmer and less effort for them to cope with.

PEDIGREE CATS

If you are determined to have a pedigree cat, then you should really contact a breeder to obtain your pet. This will not be cheap, depending on how many 'faults' your chosen cat has and how good its pedigree is. Breeders can be found through their advertisements in cat magazines, through your local cat club or via the G.C.C.F. (see Appendix for their address).

You should always visit breeders first, so that you can see their premises and discuss exactly what you are looking for. Do bear in mind that many popular breeders have waiting lists for their kittens, so you may not be able to make an 'instant' or even an 'imminent' purchase.

Unless you have plenty of time to spare for grooming your pet, a long-haired variety is probably not the best choice. They do look absolutely wonderful with their long, flowing hair, but these cats need assistance in keeping their coats tangle-free and in top condition. A Long-Hair with a dirty, matted coat will soon become a very miserable animal. Long-Hairs will also shed a fair amount of hair around the house during the moulting season, so if this would be a problem for you, choose a short-haired variety.

If you have children, be selective in choosing your pet. You will need to bring home a cat which will settle in easily and will be tolerant of quite a lot of human contact and handling. Sometimes a cat which has been brought up in a breeder's cattery rather than a home environment can be shy of humans and too reserved to cope with boisterous children. Do talk to your breeder about this and make sure that you don't end up purchasing the wrong kitten. A timid animal will not settle in properly to a typical noisy home environment, and this could be an unhappy experience for all of you.

NON-PEDIGREE OR CROSS-BRED CATS

If you are willing to consider a cat which is cross-bred, or a so-called 'moggie', then there are many more options open to you. Other owners may well be advertising kittens as 'free to good homes'. Your local vet's surgery is a good place to look for advertisements, as well as your newsagent and local paper. It is even better if you can obtain a kitten from someone you know, especially when you know that the mother cat is a happy, healthy one from a good home.

Never agree to have a kitten unseen, purely on the strength of an advertisement. You should always arrange to visit, so that you can see the home, the mother and the rest of the litter, as well as the kitten you are interested in.

PET SHOPS

Pet shops are another source of cross-bred kittens, though a less ideal one. They rarely have pedigree kittens available. The problem with pet shops is that kittens from different litters are often mixed up, in what is a strange and confusing environment for them.

There is no way for you to tell what sort of home they came from, or how healthy their mother and the rest of the litter were. (And all of these questions are vitally important when judging the health and future temperament of a new kitten.) If you must acquire your kitten this way, then examine it especially carefully, and be on your guard for any warning signs of illness.

CAT REFUGES

It is definitely a good deed to take a cat or kitten from a cats' refuge, and of course this is also cheaper than buying one. However, depending on what sort of background it has had previously, it may be emotionally disturbed, in poor physical condition or at the very least take longer to settle down than you might normally expect.

It is sensible to discuss your home situation with those running the refuge, so that they can help you to make a suitable choice. A cat (particularly an adult) which has had a disturbed background may settle better with an owner who is used to cats, rather than with someone who is new to cat ownership.

A cat from a refuge will also need a thorough health check from your vet, who should also be able to tell you whether or not it has been neutered, and make some sort of a reasonable guess as to its age. It is a good idea to get it vaccinated and wormed as soon as you bring it home with you, because there is no guarantee that it will have had the correct health care in the past, and you don't want to start off with problems.

CHOOSING YOUR CAT OR KITTEN

Often a particular animal will catch your eye and you will set your heart on having that one, but before you decide finally, do

Fig. 19. Choose a healthy kitten.

check for the obvious signs of good health.

Your cat or kitten should be bright-eyed and alert, with no trace of discharges from the eyes or nose and no sneezing or coughing apparent. If the animal you are looking at has a runny nose and is sneezing, don't believe it if the owner tells you it's 'just a cold'. Cats rarely get colds, but they do get cat 'flu, and it is generally very serious when they do. So, beware of any sneezing or coughing cats, because they are probably about to become very ill. (You should also avoid any others kept with them; even if they do not show symptoms they are probably incubating the disease and will develop it later.)

Next, examine the ears. They should look clean and healthy, with no dark brown ear wax visible, or any crusty deposits which could indicate the presence of ear mites. An infestation of ear mites can be cured by a vet, but it can make cats (and especially kittens) quite ill, so it is best to avoid any animal you see with this sort of condition.

The cat's coat is the next thing to check. It should be clean and shiny, with no thin patches or bits of flea dirt present. (Flea dirt just looks like black specks of powder in the coat.) Fleas can be treated fairly easily with a good dusting of flea powder, and it is probably not a bad idea to give your new cat or kitten a preventative treatment of this when you bring it home anyway, just in case.

If you are choosing a kitten, have a look at the shape of its abdomen. A slightly rounded shape is fine and healthy (you don't want a kitten whose ribs are showing), but a very rounded stomach can indicate the presence of roundworms. This probably means that the mother and the kittens were not properly dosed with worm tablets at the appropriate time, and you should be dubious about the health of the whole litter.

The final health check is to ensure that your kitten has no sign of lameness or other deformity. It should be able to walk, run and jump quite happily and it should appear generally active and interested in what is going on around it.

Sexing the Kitten
It can be surprisingly difficult to tell the difference between male and female kittens. The best way is to find an example of each and look at them side by side; the differences between the two can then be seen more easily.

As there is no external penis in a cat, the key indicator is the distance between the openings of the body underneath the tail. In a male kitten there is a much greater distance between these openings.

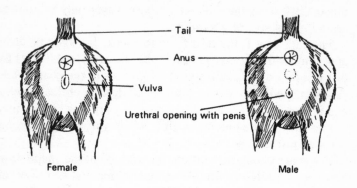

**Fig. 20.   The male and female anatomy of a kitten.
Note the difference in distance between the
anus and the vulva or penis.**

Personality Traits

The final thing which you need to observe before deciding on
a new pet is its personality. With an adult cat you will be able
to tell a lot about it from how it responds to you or its current
owner. If it is aggressive, or withdrawn, it may not settle with
you and you could have problems later on.

However, you must make allowances for the fact that you are
a complete stranger to it and an adult cat will always be a little
reserved with anyone new. If in doubt, ask questions about its
behaviour and background (although in the case of adopting a
cat from a refuge, these may not be known).

A kitten should be much less cautious with new people than
an adult cat and should let you handle it quite readily. The best
indicator of its personality is to observe how it behaves with

its brothers and sisters, so take a good look at the whole litter. All of them should be active and playful, with a natural curiosity about their environment, and they should all look healthy.

The size of the kittens is not particularly important when it comes to choosing one for a pet. It really only matters to breeders if they are trying to produce a certain size of individual. The fact that a certain kitten may be smaller than some of its fellows does not mean that there is anything wrong with it, or that it will make a less good pet. It is absolutely normal for some individuals in a litter to be smaller than others.

It is far more important to notice if one of the kittens has a very aggressive personality. If it appears to be bullying the others, hissing and spitting and throwing its weight about, then avoid it. It will not make a good pet. Similarly, if one of the kittens appears very withdrawn and reluctant to be handled, then the likelihood is that it will never enjoy living in a household with children and having a lot of human contact. Pay particular attention if it appears to be startled by sudden noises − this is a sure sign of a nervous temperament. Avoid this one if you have children or a dog at home.

The ideal kitten will be happy with its brothers and sisters and will play normally with them. It will also respond to your attempts to play with it, or handle it, and it will take a keen interest in anything going on around it. A curious, adventurous kitten is a good sign; this one will probably be intelligent and quick to adapt to its new surroundings.

One or Two?
Is it better to have one cat or two? (Or even more, if you have the space available?) This is a difficult question to answer, since it depends on so many different factors. The first one is really your home environment. If you live in a flat, or near a busy road and you have to keep your cat indoors most of the time, then it is not going to be able to mix freely with other cats in the area.

If you add to this an owner who is out a lot of the time, for example at work, then obviously a second cat will be great company for the first one, who otherwise would be left alone for much of the time. Although a cat will cope quite well with long periods alone, often snoozing for much of it, there is no doubt that two cats of a similar age can have a great deal of fun playing together. This would occupy many happy hours for them while you were out.

If you consider having two cats, then be aware of the territorial aspects to this decision, too. It is far better to acquire two cats at the same time, and ideally two of the same age. Try to get two littermates if at all possible, because they will already be used to each other. They will then happily settle into their new home together. The worst thing you could do would be to allow one cat to establish its territory in your house and then introduce another one later. The original cat would be very likely to resent the 'intruder' and there would be battles until they could reach a compromise in dividing up the house between them.

Of course, even with littermates, in some cases you may still find that they only tolerate each other and will generally find their own space to live in, avoiding each other as much as possible. You may also find the occasional low-key fight going on in your home if they have a disagreement. This is all part of normal cat behaviour and is nothing to be over-concerned about.

If you *are* considering having two cats, then you also have to take into account that any costs associated with the cat such as feeding, cat litter, boarding fees and vaccination fees will be doubled. Although cats are reasonably cheap to feed, these costs can mount up and it is best to be sure that you can afford them before committing yourself.

If your home is one where it is easy to fit a cat-flap and allow a cat access to the surrounding area, then one cat will settle in perfectly happily and will go out and amuse itself during the day. It will also mix with other cats in the neighbourhood if it wants to. In this case, there is really no special advantage to having a second cat unless you particularly want two. As you can see, there are no hard and fast rules about having one cat as opposed to two or more. It is really a question of choice, depending on your individual circumstances.

5

CARING FOR YOUR CAT

BASIC EQUIPMENT

A cat's needs are fairly simple, but there are a few pieces of basic equipment which you will require before bringing your new pet home with you. The first item is, of course, a cat basket to carry it home in. It is no use thinking that you can just hold the cat in your arms; the likelihood is that it will become frightened, struggle, escape from you and run off, never to be seen again. You must make sure that the cat is securely contained in some kind of carrier, especially if you are travelling home by car.

Many cats can become quite anxious in a car, and if not confined to a basket can go wild, becoming a real danger to the driver. Always keep the windows closed while travelling by car; the loud noise from an open car window can terrify even experienced cat travellers, resulting in total panic. This usually means you end up with the poor cat fouling its bedding and probably the car too.

Cat Carrier

At a pinch, a cardboard box with a lid on it will make a cat carrier as long as you make plenty of air holes in the sides and top, and secure it firmly with string. Most vets also sell similar cardboard carriers quite cheaply. However, cats loathe being imprisoned inside a dark, stuffy box and forcing them into it will only increase their level of panic. So, if you can afford one, it is really better to get a proper cat basket from your local pet shop. These are generally available in plastic or in wicker, and they have a grille front through which the cat can breathe and see what is going on around it. There is a carrying handle on the top for easy lifting, and a hinged door for easy access. Make sure that it is large enough for the cat to stand up and turn around in.

You should line the box or basket with something warm and soft for the cat to sit on. Although this will not work the first time that you bring a new cat home, subsequently it can be a good idea to pick something which will smell reassuringly of the cat and its home, to make the whole experience less frightening. (For example, you could try a blanket from the bed which it normally sleeps in.)

When you are bringing your new pet home, it may help it to tolerate the journey better if it can travel on someone's knee. They can then stroke the cat through the grille of the cat basket, which should soothe it if it becomes nervous.

A Bed for your Cat

The next piece of equipment which you will need is a bed for the cat to sleep in. Although you may find that your cat will choose to sleep in other places as well, it is important to establish a place for sleeping which your cat can identify as its own. This will help it to settle down faster in a new home. Putting the bed somewhere warm will also please your cat since cats like nothing better than snoozing in a warm corner.

The cheapest way of providing your cat with a good, snug bed is to make your own, using a cardboard box without a lid. It will make it easier for your cat to get in and out if you cut away half of one side, especially if it is a smallish kitten. Leave the other sides as they are, because the high sides around it will give the cat a sense of security.

The box then needs to be lined with some warm material, such as an old blanket or towel. Don't forget that you will have to change this lining and wash it every so often, since your cat will probably groom itself there, leaving a gradual build-up of dirt and cat fur.

If you decide to *buy* a bed for your cat, then any pet shop will have a wide selection for you to look at. There will probably be shaped beds of various sizes, both wicker and plastic, usually open, and also thick cotton ones which are usually enclosed at the top with a front entrance. The latter are often fleecy-lined. All of these would be highly acceptable to your new pet.

When choosing between them, you should consider firstly where the bed is going to be kept. If it is going to be very much on show, then you might want to choose a more expensive bed such as a wicker one with an attractive appearance. However, this will be a lot less easy to clean than a similar plastic one which you could disinfect easily if necessary. Wicker and plastic beds will usually need to be lined in the same way as a home-made bed would, although in some cases they are sold with a fitted, padded liner. Do check that the liner is washable before purchasing one of these, because it will soon get dirty. If the room where the bed is going to be kept gets cold at night in the winter, then a fleecy-lined, enclosed bed may be the best choice. (Before buying, check that the one you have chosen is washable; most good ones are.)

If you are buying a bed for a kitten, don't be tempted to buy one of the cute-looking small beds which are sold especially for kittens, unless you don't mind the fact that your kitten will outgrow it in a matter of months. It is better economy to buy a full-size one which will last a lifetime.

Litter Tray

The next item you will need to purchase is a sturdy litter tray. Even if you are planning to let your new pet go out regularly and use the garden rather than a litter tray inside, you will still need to buy one. When you first bring your new cat or kitten home, you will have to keep it indoors until it is accustomed to its surroundings, so you will have to train it to use a litter tray during this time. In any case, it is as well to be sure that your cat is familiar with a litter tray, because at certain times in its life it is bound to have to use one, e.g. during a stay at a cattery. Equally, if it is ever unwell, or the weather is particularly foul, then you may need to keep it indoors.

There are a number of different types of litter tray available from pet shops and larger supermarkets. They are generally fairly cheap and are made out of good, strong plastic. Although they are usually made to a fairly standard size, they do vary in depth, so be aware that it is better to buy one more than 5cm (2″) deep. Cats will usually bury their faeces in the litter, and the sides of the shallow variety do not adequately contain the spare litter which is kicked up during this process. Try to get a tray which is about 9cm (3½″) deep, otherwise you will spend a lot of time sweeping up cat litter from the surrounding area.

It is quite a good idea to line the area around the tray with newspaper or kitchen towel while your cat is getting used to the new tray. Sometimes, particularly with new kittens, their aim is not entirely accurate. The paper will protect the floor area and can be easily disposed of and replaced as necessary.

There are various types of cat litter available from shops and supermarkets, all of which are effective. Some have a built-in deodorant which can be useful, but this is not vital if the litter is changed regularly. Bear in mind that you *must* change the litter when it is soiled; cats are very clean creatures and often will refuse to use a dirty litter tray, which can lead to 'accidents' elsewhere in the home.

The best method of changing the litter is to use one of the plastic scoops made for the purpose. You use the scoop to remove the soiled litter from the tray and dispose of it, then you can fill the space which is left with fresh litter. This is more economical than replacing the whole trayful of litter each time. Remember to disinfect both the tray and the scoop from time to time, preferably after the cat has just used the tray so it won't object to its removal for a few minutes. Alternatively, you could purchase two trays and alternate them. Do make sure that the tray is thoroughly dry before using it again and check that there is no disinfectant on it which could be transferred to the cat.

There are various weights of cat litter available. The lighter variety is less heavy to carry around, but can be more dusty and powdery. The heavyweight variety is more solid and will create less dust. Both are effective and absorbent.

Feeding Bowls

Feeding bowls are the next item you will require for your cat. The minimum you will need is two bowls: one for water or milk and one for food. Bowls are preferable to saucers because they are much less likely to tip up. There are specially non-tip varieties available from supermarkets and pet shops which are inexpensive. They will last a long time, particularly if you buy the unbreakable plastic ones. You can also use old crockery for this if you don't want to buy new bowls, but you should remember to keep them separate from the rest of your china for hygiene reasons.

Brushes and Combs

Many people labour under the false impression that cats require no additional grooming by their owners. This is untrue, although the amount of assistance required does vary tremendously between long-haired and short-haired breeds. Short-haired cats do keep themselves in good shape as a rule, but they will benefit from extra help during moulting. Long-Hairs will need daily attention.

The basic tools required are a soft, nylon brush (available from pet shops and supermarkets, or a soft hairbrush could be used) and a fine steel comb. In the case of a long-haired cat, you may also need a pair of small scissors for the removal of any clumps of matted hair which cannot be untangled.

INTRODUCING A KITTEN TO ITS NEW HOME

When you first bring your new kitten home, it is likely to be bewildered by all the new sights and sounds, and more than a little frightened. However, as with all young things, eventually curiosity will take over and it will be unable to resist the temptation to explore. This is all part of the settling in process.

It is best to begin by putting your kitten, its bed, litter tray and food dishes all in one room and allowing it to get to know its way about. You can then introduce it to further rooms gradually, once it has established a 'home base'. (The same principles apply to an adult cat, when it is brought to a new home for the first time.)

If, when you allow it to explore (or even when you first bring it home) it climbs up on to the top of a high wardrobe or cupboard and refuses to come down again, don't panic. Your cat is feeling insecure and by getting as high as possible it is making itself feel safer. This is quite a common reaction and nothing to worry about. Don't scare the cat further by trying to grab it or coax it down. Leave it in peace and it will come down when it is ready, probably when it becomes really hungry.

If you have children and/or a dog, don't introduce all of them to your frightened kitten straightaway. Do it gradually, and in this way you will be building up its confidence. Although your kitten will love playing with the children once it has settled, try to ensure that it is given some peace and quiet to come to terms with its new location before they deluge it with affection and rough and tumble games.

Explain to them that kittens are quite young and fragile, and so need to be handled gently. Be especially careful to teach them how to lift a cat, making sure that the hind quarters are supported. If they try to lift it by the top of its body only, it will be very uncomfortable and is likely to struggle and scratch to get free. This will not help it to form a good relationship with your children, so it is best to make sure that it doesn't happen.

Once the kitten has gained a little confidence, you could try giving your children a cat toy so that they can start to play with their new pet. A ball of wool, or a ball of tinfoil on a string, is ideal. Pet shops also sell a variety of toys such as catnip mice which can be fun. Playing together will help children to get used to the kitten and accustom the kitten to them.

Remind them not to shout loudly or move suddenly; both of these will frighten the kitten and if they do it often, it will start to associate the children with fear and will run away from them. Children get very upset if this happens with their new pet! Teach them to walk up to it slowly and quietly, then stroke it, so that it will associate them with pleasure and fun instead of fear.

In the case of a resident dog, the introduction will be more difficult. Keep the kitten away from the dog for the first day or so until it is reasonably settled, then pick a good time to introduce them, for example, when the dog has been fed and is quite docile; perhaps when it is lying in front of the fire in the evening. Carry your kitten into the room with you and sit down with it on your lap. Hold it firmly, so that it can't get off to a bad start by running towards the door as soon as it sees the dog. The dog would be bound to chase it, and this wouldn't be the best way to begin their relationship.

Make sure that your dog stays at floor level and the kitten stays with you; it will feel safer at a higher level than the dog. If the dog comes over to look at the kitten, this is fine as long as it isn't aggressive towards it. Eventually, after a few days of holding the kitten while it is in the same room as the dog, you will be able to try putting it down on to the floor. Keep a close watch for trouble starting initially, but if no fights occur after a day or two, the two animals have probably accepted each other. You should also be careful to feed them in different places and at different times, otherwise you may find that one tries to eat the other's food. This would not be good for their health or their tolerance of each other. Once they have become used to each other, cats and dogs will generally co-exist quite happily, although they can occasionally be rather jealous of each other and compete for their owner's attention. Try to minimise this by making an equal fuss of both of them.

FEEDING

Do find out what your pet has been eating in its previous home, because this is what it will be used to. Offering it something different when it is already in a strange environment may cause it to refuse food. In any case, when you first bring your new cat or kitten home, it may be too unsettled to eat anything.

Try offering it a tiny amount of some extremely tasty food such as chopped, cooked chicken or white fish, to tempt it. If it eats this small portion, then you can give it more. Getting your cat or kitten to eat in its new surroundings is a major hurdle; once it does this, it is half-way towards accepting its new home. If you can persuade it to eat, and it then washes itself and uses the litter tray, you are virtually home and dry.

You should always feed your cat in the same place, because cats appreciate routine and familiarity. (The only exception to this is when you have a new arrival; you may need to confine it to one room while it settles in.)

What to feed it

If possible, it is a good idea to continue to feed your cat in the same way as its previous owner. Cats are often very fussy about particular brands of tinned food, and when they are accustomed to one it can be hard to make them change to another. Similarly, you may notice that your cat shows a dislike for a particular flavour, in which case it is best to avoid that.

As far as health and nutrition are concerned, all proprietary cat foods are designed specifically to cater for the unique balance of proteins, fats, vitamins and minerals which your cat requires. As such, they are all suitable foods for you to give to your pet, and they can be supplemented with occasional treats such as roast meat or poultry, or fish.

You cannot feed a cat exclusively on scraps of human food such as meat or white fish, because this won't give it all the nutrients it requires for an active, healthy life. Neither can it be fed on the same tinned food which you give to your dog. Cat food may very well look and smell similar to dog food, but it is not the same in terms of the balance of nutrients. Dogs require a different diet from cats.

Try to feed your cat or kitten around the same time each day, preferably twice daily. (If your kitten is less than six months old, it will require feeding more frequently, probably three or four times a day.) A kitten will consume an amazing amount of food for its size; this is because it is growing so quickly. Give it a decent-sized bowlful of food and see whether it all gets eaten. If any is left, then you have probably overestimated the quantity by that amount.

It is a very bad habit to leave food down all day for cats to pick at when they feel like it. It is much better to feed them at the proper time and remove the bowl when they have finished, disposing of any leftovers. This will not only train them to eat a sensible amount at once, but it will also avoid the hygiene problem of half-eaten dishes of cat food lying around in your house. If you have a dog, leaving cat food out can mean that the dog begins snacking on the leftovers, so it really is better to remove it.

A large bone (such as a lamb bone) will be a treat for your pet, and it will happily chew and suck at the bits of meat and bone marrow. Never give your cat small bones such as chicken bones though, because these can splinter causing the cat to choke. You can also give it crunchy cat biscuits, either alone or mixed with other moist food. You *must* make sure that the cat doesn't eat too much dry food at once though, otherwise it may be sick. Try to make sure that it drinks at the same time, and never offer it dry cat biscuits without a drink as well. See also page 22.

DRINKING

Cats take in most of the moisture they require from their food, and they do not as a rule drink a great deal. However, you should always make sure that fresh water is available for them, or milk if they are reluctant to drink water. Cats like pure water and sometimes will refuse to drink tap water because of the chlorine and fluoride added to it. In this case you could try giving them filtered or bottled water, or milk (preferably not whole milk because this can be slightly too rich for their stomachs).

GROOMING

Grooming is a part of cat care which both cats and their owners generally enjoy. You should start at the cat's head and work slowly down the back and tail, followed by the cat's stomach and legs. Begin by using a steel comb to remove any tangles or matted hair. If there are any knots which are impossibly tangled (and unfortunately this can happen in a Long-Hair, especially under the chin), then you will need to snip these out with your small scissors. Be very careful to hold the cat securely during this procedure, to be sure that the scissors do not graze the cat's skin if it wriggles about. (This is really a two-person job because it is very difficult to hold a cat firmly and cut tangles at the same time.)

Next, follow the same route with your soft brush to remove any remaining loose hairs from the coat. While you are doing this, have a good look at the coat, checking for any injuries, signs of fleas or ear mites. Grooming is an ideal opportunity to give the cat a thorough inspection, and if you do this while it is being brushed it will rarely object.

VACCINATION

Before you bring your new cat or kitten home, it is vital to find out what it has already been inoculated against. The correct practice is for kittens to have been inoculated before they leave their mother for a new home, but this is not always done and you should make sure that you find out whether yours has been treated. If the kitten has not been vaccinated, then you must arrange to have this done immediately. The same applies to an adult cat.

There are two main diseases which can kill cats and these

are the ones against which your pet must be vaccinated every year. They are gastro-enteritis and cat 'flu. Your vet will be able to arrange a vaccination for your cat and this can generally be done with a single, combined injection. Cats are not usually upset by having an injection (unlike some humans) and it does give them very effective protection against these two lethal viruses. Kittens may usually be vaccinated after they reach nine weeks old.

As you can imagine, viral infections can spread like wildfire through a boarding cattery, so you will be expected to produce a current certificate of vaccination when you take your cat in to board. Similarly, if you take your cat to a breeder for mating purposes, you will also be asked to show that your cat is immune to these two diseases.

WORMING

The other regular preventative measure you will need to organise straightaway is worming. Unfortunately cats can pick up intestinal worms quite easily, particularly if they are good hunters, and the only way to ensure that these don't become a health hazard is to dose your cat with suitable worm tablets regularly.

If you have just acquired a kitten, do check that it has been properly wormed in its previous home. If you can find out the exact date, you will then know when to give it a further dose of tablets yourself. If you cannot find out, and it appears that the kitten has not been treated, you should start immediately. Worms can interfere with the digestion of a kitten to such an extent that it can become quite ill, and even die in severe cases. You should also start treatment straightaway for an adult cat whose history is not known, although for adults intestinal worms are less of a danger and more of a nuisance than anything else. However, as the worms live on food in the cat's gut, obviously if left untreated they can cause poor health and discomfort to the animal.

Although cats are clean creatures and pose less of a risk than dogs, if an occasional worm or worm segment is shed by the cat then it could be transferred to humans. This is especially likely to affect children who tend to spend more time with their faces and hands on the floor. So, it is obviously very desirable to prevent your cat from carrying worms in the first place.

There are a number of different tablets available for this purpose, all of which carry full instructions on how many to give your cat or kitten (dependent on body weight). You can also buy combination packs which will treat the cat for roundworm and tapeworm. Usually these contain a course of tablets to be given once a week over a three week period. It is important to complete the course at the right time, otherwise the tablets may prove ineffective. Vets, pet shops and some large supermarkets now carry stocks of these tablets, and it is sensible to worm your cat with them every six months.

COLLARS AND NAME TAGS

Does a cat really need a collar? It is a subject about which owners can argue endlessly, but the answer is really that it depends on the cat and its habits. One of the benefits of a collar is that you can attach a small cat tag to it, carrying your name and address, so that if your cat gets itself lost or is injured, then you can be easily traced.

The drawback of a collar is that if your cat loves to climb trees, it can become trapped if a branch gets stuck underneath the collar. Sadly, cats have choked to death in the past, while trying to free themselves from this predicament.

You can limit the risk of this happening by buying a collar made of soft material rather than leather, and one which is also elasticated, so that the cat cannot choke itself. However, it could still fall from a tree and be strangled if the collar caught on a branch. This is probably a smaller risk than the chance of your cat getting run over if you live near a busy road, so you may still decide in favour of a collar, all things considered.

When fitting a collar to your cat, make sure that you can insert a finger underneath it, between it and the cat's neck. This will ensure that it is not too tight. Make sure that it is not too loose either; if you can get two fingers underneath it, then it needs to be tightened. Don't leave any excess length flapping about at the end of it, in case this gets stuck in something or hinders the cat when it is moving around.

Flea Collars

Flea collars are an extremely useful invention, especially as most cats hate flea powders and sprays so it can be difficult to treat them thoroughly. Flea collars are usually made of felt impregnated with a chemical which kills fleas. As fleas love to settle around the cat's neck, a flea collar is a good way of preventing them from using your pet as a host.

The collars are generally effective for between two and four months, depending on the brand. Keep watch on your cat's neck for any sign of irritation, because some flea collars can cause an allergic reaction. If this happens, remove the collar immediately. If the reaction does not subside in a day or two, consult your vet.

Waterproof collars (usually plastic) are also available, but these smell appalling and will probably be detested by your cat and all who share a room with it. Unless your cat enjoys getting wet (and not many do) you probably do not require a waterproof flea collar.

The main flea season is summer when the weather gets warm, so you will probably need to put a collar on your cat in May and replace it when necessary. The risk of fleas should have lessened by the end of September, as the weather cools down again.

Do not be tempted to leave a flea collar on your cat outside the main flea season 'just in case'. The chemicals in the collar may very well upset your cat's skin if worn over a long period, and there is also a strong possibility that they will affect its coat. This can result in an ugly bald patch where the collar has been, and in some cases the fur will never grow back again. So make sure that your cat's neck is given a rest from the collar during the winter.

SAFETY

Although your kitten may appear as if it is well able to fend for itself, it is nevertheless a young, inexperienced animal still learning about the world. For this reason, there are a few simple precautions which you will need to take to prevent it from getting itself into trouble.

The first is to introduce it to your home environment gradually, being sure that there are no open windows or doors out of which it could run and get lost. Make sure that you don't leave any cupboard or wardrobe door open, especially the airing cupboard. A young kitten could easily get trapped inside and suffocate. Also make sure that toilet-seat lids are kept down, so that an over-curious kitten cannot topple in and be unable to get out again. Always keep the doors of front-loading washing machines closed, particularly if there is a load of dry clothing inside, waiting to be washed. A pile of clothes is an attractive place to sleep for a small kitten.

Never leave your kitten unattended near an open window; kittens do not have a proper sense of height until they are almost adult and so can sometimes misjudge a jump and be injured by the fall.

An adult cat will be much more worldly-wise, but you will still need to keep it indoors for a few days until it has had time to adjust to its new surroundings and to living with you. After about a week if it seems happy and contented, it is probably safe to let it go outside with you.

Introduce it to your back garden first. This will be sufficient to begin with, and your cat will probably spend a long time sniffing everything to get its bearings. It may appear rather fearful to begin with, but this should soon wear off as it begins to learn its way around.

As soon as it gains confidence, your cat will be off over the nearest fence to establish its territory in next door's garden. Don't be concerned; it is not likely to stray too far from home initially. After a short exploration it will be back to base to check that it has got its directions right.

If you have a kitten and you feel that it has fully settled after about ten days with you, you can introduce it to the world outside the back door. It is best to do this gradually though, keeping a very close eye on it at first and making sure that it stays within the confines of your garden.

GOING OUT AT NIGHT

On no account should you let a kitten out at night. It is too small to cope with being out in the cold for so long and is probably also too young to defend itself against other large cats or foxes which may be out and about. The risk of being run over is also much greater at night, because the average motorist will not be able to see a tiny kitten in the darkness.

An adult cat can be left out at night if it has access to somewhere dry and out of the wind, such as a garden shed or garage. You could try fitting a cat-flap for it, so that it can shelter inside if the weather turns nasty. A cat should not be turned out at night and left to fend for itself with no shelter.

NAMING

Choosing a name for your cat or kitten is largely a matter of personal preference, but do be aware that cats understand their names and can be reluctant to change them. So, if you adopt an adult cat, then you may have to adopt its name as well. If you really cannot bear the original name, then you *can* teach the cat to answer to another one, given time and patience, but you should not expect overnight results.

A kitten, on the other hand, will learn a new name very quickly indeed, and will soon come when called. You can teach it to do this by making a big fuss of it when it comes to you in response to its name being called. (With an adult cat learning a new name, you may have to bribe it with titbits of food, until it learns what is required.)

A three-syllable name (e.g. Clau-di-a) will be learned faster than a two-syllable name (e.g. Nel-son). This is for the simple reason that most of our everyday speech is in one or two syllables, rather than three. So, the only time that the cat will hear these three associated sounds is when we are using its name. It will very soon learn to identify with those sounds.

Cats respond to tone of voice and pitch, rather than actual words, so the way in which you say its name is also important, particularly at first. Try always to say the name in the same way when you call.

If children are choosing a name for the kitten, try to make sure that they choose something suitable. It is all very well to pick a cute name for a small, cuddly kitten, but by the time that the kitten grows up into a beefy tom cat it can be very inappropriate. Remember that you are going to be the one who looks silly calling out 'Tinkerbell', or similar, as the largest, most aggressive cat in the neighbourhood crashes out of the bushes to come home for his tea.

OBEDIENCE

Never be tempted to smack your cat to make it obey you. This will only make it become nervous and fearful, and that much more reluctant to form a bond of affection with you. Cats understand tone of voice extremely well and they detest loud noises, so it is usually quite sufficient to raise your voice and say 'No' firmly. If the 'No' needs reinforcing, then a loud clap of the hands will generally work.

If your pet goes somewhere you don't want it to, such as on a table top, lift it down immediately and say 'No' at the same time. Then if it shows signs of trying to get up there again, repeat the 'No' to deter it. You may have to do this several times, until it learns. The important thing is always to reinforce what is forbidden. It is no good allowing the cat to do certain things on some occasions and not on others; this is far too confusing for it. You must be consistent. Eventually, it will learn what you don't want it to do.

TOILET-TRAINING

If you are fortunate enough to have a kitten which has been kept with its mother until it is nine weeks old, it will probably have been toilet-trained already. If not, then you will have to teach it. The key to this is not to frighten the kitten by shouting at it (this will only make accidents more likely).

Until it has the knack of using the litter tray properly, keep the kitten in one room. If it has the freedom of the house, it may forget where the tray is, or it may not have acquired sufficient control of its bladder to wait until it can get to it. This can result in urine on the carpet. The problem with this is that the strong smell will then encourage the kitten to return to that spot for the same purpose. If accidents *do* occur, disinfect the area thoroughly and keep the kitten well away from it until it is fully toilet-trained.

It can often help to place the kitten on the litter tray after it has eaten, and walk its front paws gently up and down, to mimic how a cat would normally dig in a tray before using it. This can also be a useful trick with an adult cat which may not have used a tray for a long time and so might be out of the habit of doing so. It will soon remember, given a bit of encouragement.

SCRATCHING

All cats scratch. They need to do it to keep their claws trim and sharp, as well as to mark their territory. It is unrealistic to expect to be able to train them out of it; you will fail. What you *can* do is to train them to scratch in an acceptable place.

The best place is undoubtedly in the garden, using a tree or fence, but failing that, there are a number of scratching pads or posts covered with sisal which you can buy for indoor use. You should train your cat to use these from as early an age as possible, otherwise it may form an unwelcome habit of using the doormat or the best Chinese rug. Habits once formed are hard to break.

STEALING FOOD

Regrettably most cats are opportunists and will steal the odd piece of food if they get the chance, particularly if it is something tasty such as chicken. The only real way to combat this is to keep food somewhere inaccessible, such as on a high worktop, under a cover. You should always train your cat not to walk along kitchen worktops for hygiene reasons, so keeping food 'out of bounds' will help. Never put plates of food down on the floor, because your cat will see this as fair game. After all, you put its food on to the floor, so it will think that it has a right to anything on that level. Be especially careful of what your cat is doing if you are barbecuing food out in the garden; it may smell the food and try to take some, not realising how hot the coals and grill are.

The only real way to combat stealing is to remove the temptation in the first place. If you cannot do this, then you need to be vigilant, so that if you see your cat making an approach to the food, you can deter it with a sharp 'No' or a clap of the hands.

6

SHOULD YOU LET YOUR CAT BREED?

MAKING AN INFORMED CHOICE

It is important not to be swayed by too much emotion when deciding whether or not to let your cat breed. There is absolutely no truth in the Old Wives' Tale that it is better for a female cat's health and temperament to let her have at least one litter of kittens, and in fact the opposite can be true. In many cases the neutered female is longer-lived and requires less medical care than a female cat (or 'queen') which is allowed to have kittens, and it will often settle more easily into a neighbourhood or family.

Equally, because an unneutered cat would be capable of having several litters each year, she could easily produce over a hundred kittens during her lifetime, which would exhaust her strength (and yours). There is also the question of how to find good homes for all those kittens. So, it is vital to decide early on how many litters of kittens you are willing to let your cat have (if any) and plan accordingly. A female cat may become mature enough to breed at anything after three and a half months old, although the average age for this is around seven months, so it is not a decision which can be delayed for long.

AN UNNEUTERED MALE

In the case of a male cat, or tom, there can also be very good reasons for considering neutering. An unneutered tom can be a very boisterous creature, always fighting and difficult to restrain from scratching and being generally aggressive. Neutering can have a calming effect without altering his basic personality and it will make life more peaceful for you and for him.

Mature male cats tend to wander far and wide in search of females, which can mean that they often end up getting lost and becoming strays, or disappearing from home for long periods of time, returning hungry and battle-scarred. They have a strong instinct to fight other males in their territory and consequently can often receive nasty wounds and scratches, coming back home in quite poor condition. Regrettably many of them also become victims of road accidents because of this tendency to wander.

There is also another disadvantage to keeping an unneutered tom as a pet. His urine will develop a strong, unpleasant and very persistent smell, and no matter how well house-trained you may think he is, in the breeding season he will spray urine over his territory. The bad news is that his territory includes your home and its furnishings. It is well nigh impossible to train him out of this, because his instinct to do it is so strong, so by far the best solution is to have him neutered.

There is also no truth in the rumour that neutering will make a cat fat, or unfit. Fat, unfit cats are a result of over-feeding and inactivity, much like fat, unfit humans. With a sensible diet and plenty of exercise your neutered- cat will remain perfectly sleek and active, as nature intended.

MATING HABITS AND REPRODUCTIVE CYCLE

If you do decide to let your cat breed, it is helpful to know what to expect in terms of behaviour. When the female kitten first becomes ready to mate, usually referred to as 'coming into season', she will start to behave very differently from normal. She will develop a very loud and persistent miaow, quite unlike her normal voice. This is known as 'calling'. However, it is not safe to rely on this as the only indicator of a cat coming into season, because some breeds (e.g. Russian Blue) may not be noticeably noisy. A female cat in season will rub and lick the areas around her vagina repeatedly, and will often be more affectionate than usual. She may also become very restless and bad-tempered, and she will probably try her hardest to get out, by any available route she can find.

Keeping a cat in at this time is not easy, because she is determined to get outside and find herself a mate. If there are any toms in the neighbourhood, you may also find a chorus of them on your roof or on your doorstep. If you have a cat-flap in your back door you will need to secure this, otherwise you may also find toms in your kitchen. If you let your cat out at this time, she will almost certainly become pregnant.

COURTSHIP AND MATING

Courtship can be a somewhat rough process, especially because the cat will not accept all suitors. Mating is a fairly brief process in itself, although it is usually repeated at frequent intervals. To indicate her willingness to mate, the female will raise her hind quarters in the air, displaying them to the male who will stalk around her. He will then mount her, generally grabbing her by the scruff of the neck and occasionally biting her.

Ovulation is brought on by the act of mating, and the number of eggs released will determine the maximum number of kittens which can be born (usually between three and six). It is perfectly possible for a cat to bear kittens from matings with different toms in the one litter, if the matings occur very closely together.

A cat will remain 'in season' for three weeks, but the symptoms will usually be especially noticeable during one of these weeks. The mating stage lasts for between twelve hours and four days, during which time the cat may not return home if she has been allowed out.

BREEDING CYCLE

The breeding period covers the majority of the year, generally from the end of December to the start of the following September, and a queen will constantly come in and out of season during this period. Most kittens are born in July and August. If they have been mated, the majority of cats will come into season again five or six weeks after the birth of the kittens, but this is by no means a totally reliable guide as some queens may become pregnant again while still suckling a litter.

SPAYING

The neutering of a female cat is known as 'spaying' and involves a surgical operation to remove both ovaries, so that the cat will not come into season again. It is performed under general anaesthetic by a veterinary surgeon. You will be asked to starve your cat for twelve hours first, to avoid the risk of vomiting, so it is probably best to keep your cat indoors for that period.

The operation is generally carried out when a cat is at least twelve weeks old, to avoid the risk of pregnancy, but opinions do vary slightly as to the best time so it is sensible to consult your vet about this first. In the case of an older cat showing signs of being in season, you will have to wait until a later date to have her spayed, because the hormonal changes in her body mean that the uterus is more fragile and prone to rupture at this time.

Complications after a spaying operation are rare. The operation is normally carried out via an incision in the flank or abdomen, after the area has been shaved of hair so that it can be kept sterile. The stitches are generally soluble so do not need to be removed.

After the Operation

It can be rather a shock to see your cat with a patch of bare pink skin and stitches, particularly when the cat itself seems rather groggy and unsteady on its feet. Try not to let this upset you and remember that it has just had a general anaesthetic. Keep it inside somewhere quiet, warm and comfortable for twenty-four hours, preferably confined to one room and you will soon start to see an improvement.

Don't be too concerned if your cat seems to want to doze and isn't particularly interested in food; it may be better to let it sleep off the anaesthetic initially. Once it shows signs of being more active you can offer it some light food such as scrambled egg or small pieces of chicken. In a couple of days your cat will be back to normal, and of course the fur will soon start to grow back again and cover the bald patch.

NEUTERING OF A MALE CAT

Neutering of a male cat is usually performed when he is between three and eight months old, although generally a male kitten will not become fully sexually mature until he is a year old. In the male cat neutering involves the removal of both testicles, and is referred to as 'castration'. The earlier that this is done the better, since the blood supply to the testicles is smaller at a younger age, and so the risk of haemorrhage after the operation is significantly reduced. If your cat is already a sexually mature adult, then it is better to have him castrated between September and December, outside the breeding season. It will be less traumatic for your cat this way, because the blood flow to the testicles is lessened at this time.

A general anaesthetic is also necessary for castration. Even though the operation is not normally an abdominal one, you can expect your cat to be weak afterwards because of the anaesthetic, so keep him indoors and let him sleep it off. Offer him a little light food and something to drink if he appears to want it.

In a few male cats one or both testicles may be retained in the abdomen rather than developing fully. In this case your vet may either advise you to wait six months and then return the cat for another examination, or if the cat is already adult he may recommend an abdominal operation. It is still advisable to have your cat neutered in such cases, because a cat with abdominal testicles will still display all the characteristics of an unneutered tom.

PREGNANCY AND GIVING BIRTH

The normal period of pregnancy is between sixty-three and sixty-six days after mating takes place. Up until five weeks afterwards there will be no real outward sign of pregnancy, though an experienced breeder or a vet may be able to detect it after about three weeks. After five or six weeks there will be some slight abdominal swelling, and the nipples may begin to enlarge, sometimes turning more pink in colour. After eight or nine weeks you may be able to see the kittens moving inside the mother's body.

Caring for your Pregnant Cat

Your cat will not need more food than usual until after her sixth week of pregnancy, and the most sensible approach is to feed her according to appetite. A pregnant queen will not usually overeat and will take what she needs gradually, until by the end of the pregnancy she will probably be consuming about twice her normal intake. It is important to make food available to her often, ideally giving her four meals a day, and it is vital to ensure that she has plenty of milk available. If your cat finds cow's milk too rich, try semi-skimmed or goat's milk. If neither of these will suit, then you must ask your vet for a calcium supplement for her.

There is no need to restrict her activity while she is pregnant, but extra care must be taken when handling her, especially during the latter stages of pregnancy. Make sure that when you lift her you support her abdomen. If you have young children, it is probably better to prevent them from picking her up at this stage. Remember that the kittens are imposing a lot of extra weight on what is quite a small animal.

About a week before the kittens are due to be born, you should dose your cat with worm tablets, to ensure that she cannot be a source of infection for the kittens. It will be necessary to repeat this treatment every week while she is suckling the kittens.

Choosing a Place for the Birth

It is important to offer your cat a choice of places to have her kittens in, otherwise she may select her own, more often than not the airing cupboard or the spare bed. About ten days before you are expecting her to give birth, start distributing strong cardboard boxes in places around the house which are warm, safe and quiet.

Choose boxes which are high sided, to give a sense of security, and which are large enough to accommodate a mother cat and several kittens. You should cut away the front of the box and make an entrance for her, but remember to leave a step of a few inches high so that tiny kittens cannot get out and wander off.

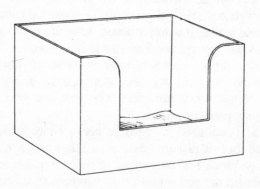

Fig. 21. A lined cardboard box with entrance step.

Line the boxes with several layers of kitchen towel to make a soft, clean bed. Provided that the room is kept warm this will be adequate bedding, and any soiled layers can be easily removed and replaced. Paper towels are much safer than cloth bedding because there is no risk of the kittens getting caught up in it and being smothered.

Labour Symptoms
As the time for her to give birth approaches, you will notice that she probably will take much more interest in one or two of the boxes than in the others. You can then remove the other ones. When it gets very near to the right time, it is a good idea to confine her to the room with the favoured box in, otherwise she may change her mind at the last minute and decide to use the spare bed after all.

You should be able to detect contractions by the movements in her sides by now and she will probably seem quite restless. She will soon go to her box and start treading down the paper to make a bed, and there may also be a slight discharge around her vagina. She may purr loudly. This is the first stage of labour.

What you should do Next
It is unusual for a cat to experience difficulty in giving birth, but it is a good idea to inform your vet when you expect it to take place just in case there are complications. Generally you should not need to interfere throughout the whole birth process, but you should monitor her progress closely, just in case your help is required.

During the next stage of labour your cat will show definite signs of straining and may cry out, particularly if this is her first litter. After a time, usually about thirty minutes, a kitten should appear and will generally pop out quite quickly. It should come out head first; if it emerges hind quarters first (a 'breech' birth) you will have to help, because this can be dangerous. There is a risk of the head getting stuck and the kitten choking. Take a clean piece of paper towel and gently manipulate the kitten out, handling it as close to the shoulders as possible to minimize injury. If the kitten appears wedged and you cannot free it easily, contact your vet without delay.

Other Possible Complications

If your cat has been straining for more than an hour without any sign of a kitten emerging, it may be that there is a kitten lying across the neck of the womb. If not corrected, this can be fatal, so call your vet immediately for assistance. It may be that a Caesarean operation is required. If this is carried out in good time before the mother becomes exhausted from straining, then she should make a good recovery and be able to rear the kittens herself. The kittens should be given back to her as soon as she recovers from the anaesthetic.

During normal labour sometimes the kitten will emerge still covered in a transparent membrane, but normally the mother should break this at once and lick the kitten to stimulate its breathing. She will then bite through the umbilical cord to sever it and in a short time the kitten will start to cry and will find its way to a nipple to suckle.

The third and final stage of labour consists of the expulsion of the afterbirth, or placenta, from the mother's body. In some cases it can be ejected still attached to the kitten and the mother will then break the connection and eat the membranes. This can look rather disgusting, but it is what normally takes place in nature and is exactly how a wild cat would behave. If your cat shows no interest in the afterbirth then it is fine to remove it, but otherwise let her eat it if she wants to.

Other kittens may be born at invervals of anything between ten minutes and an hour, each followed by an afterbirth, or you may find that the stages are mixed; e.g. two kittens followed by two afterbirths. Remember carefully to count how many afterbirths are passed, because it is most important to make sure that an afterbirth is passed for each kitten. If any are retained within the body of your cat then you will need to consult your vet, because it can lead to infection and serious illness.

You must also observe her to make sure that she does bite through the umbilical cord and also break through the transparent sac covering the kitten. If she does not, then you must assist rapidly or the young kitten will die. You can break through the membrane sac with clean fingers and you should also make sure that the kitten's nose and mouth are wiped clean. Open its mouth with one finger to stimulate the lungs into action. If you cannot see the kitten starting to breathe, hold it upside down and then gently rub its rib cage. Be careful not to apply too much pressure in case you damage any internal organs.

If the cord has not been broken by the mother after about ten minutes, then you can do this. Wash your hands with a disinfectant solution and tie a tight piece of cotton around the cord (sewing thread which has been previously boiled is ideal) making sure that it is several inches away from the kitten's abdomen. Using a pair of scissors (which you have also steri- lised by boiling) cut the cord on the side away from the knot.

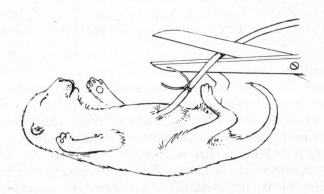

Fig. 22. Cutting the umbilical cord.

A few drops of blood may be seen, but this is no cause for alarm provided that the cord is tied off properly. The cord will shrivel up later and can be trimmed if necessary. Return the kitten to its mother straightaway so that it can begin suckling.

In some rare cases (usually where a mother cat has had to strain excessively during birth) the womb can be expelled at the end of the birth process. It will look like a red, spongy mass of flesh hanging outside the mother's body. If this happens, you must contact a vet immediately to have the womb cleaned and put back inside her body in the correct position.

After the birth
Once the litter is complete (normally between three and six kittens), the mother cat will wash them all and settle down to sleep. It is not usual for her to eat or drink during the birth, but if you offer her a drink of milk and a little food now she will probably accept it gratefully. You will need to take it to her, because she will be reluctant to leave her kittens.

Some cats will refuse to move at all, even for food or to relieve themselves. If this happens, it is worth putting a litter tray near at hand and lifting your cat out of the box and on to it, to avoid extra soiling of the bedding and possible infection to the kittens. This will also provide you with an opportunity to examine the kittens and change any bedding if necessary.

Mastitis
Once the kittens have started to suckle, keep a watch for any sign of inflammation around the milk glands. The most common ones to develop problems are those nearest the tail and often only one will be affected. It will appear red and painful and the mother will usually push away any kitten attempting to suckle from it. This is a symptom of infected milk glands, or 'mastitis', which should be treated with antibiotics from your vet as soon as possible.

Caring for the Mother Cat and Kittens

All kittens are born with their eyes closed and so are totally dependent on their mother at first. They will begin to open their eyes from five to twelve days after their birth, but she will care for them completely during the first month of their lives. She will not only feed them, but will lick them constantly to keep them clean and stimulate the normal working of their bladders and bowels.

After about three weeks she will begin toilet training them, so you should provide a litter tray for their use after they are about two and a half weeks old. You need to do this in plenty of time, otherwise they may start using a corner of the room for this purpose and develop a habit which will then be hard to break.

Keep a careful watch on the kittens to make sure that their eyes do not become sealed again with discharge. If they do, there is a risk of infection and possible damage to their eyes. Bathe them with a little cotton wool soaked in warm water to remove any discharge which you can see.

Also check to see that all the kittens are suckling properly. If one seems unable to suckle, particularly if there are signs of milk running from its nostrils, then it probably has a cleft palate and should be taken to a vet. Unfortunately this condition is incurable and once it is confirmed, the kitten is likely to have to be destroyed.

In order to feed her litter adequately without any deterioration in her own condition, the mother cat will have to consume large quantities of food and must now be fed on demand. She is also likely to drink a lot more, because of the loss of fluid involved in producing milk for her young.

Weaning

By the time they are three weeks old, the kittens will have begun to take their first tentative steps and you can now begin to wean them on to solid food. It is important to begin weaning as soon as possible, otherwise your mother cat will begin to lose condition. The easiest method of ensuring that kittens receive all the vitamins and minerals which they require is to feed them one of the proprietary canned foods for kittens now available. The balance of nutrients is different from that necessary for an adult cat, so a food designed for kittens is far more suitable to give than the same food which you give to the mother. They will also enjoy an occasional meal of mashed boiled fish or minced cooked chicken.

Try giving your kittens food on a plate rather than in a bowl at first; they often find a bowl difficult to eat from until they have grown a little larger. Milk should also be readily available, and you should supervise feeding to make sure that one or two kittens do not monopolise the food at the expense of the others.

The mother should not be allowed to eat the kittens' food either, and it may be best to put her food in a different part of the room and feed her and them simultaneously. By the time that they are five weeks old, each kitten should be capable of eating 70g (3 oz) of food a day, spread between four meals. Their mother's milk should dry up naturally once they stop suckling.

Becoming Independent

As soon as the kittens start to leave their mother, they should be placed on the litter tray after every feed to encourage them to become house trained.

When they reach the age of eight weeks, the kittens will be virtually independent of their mother, and she may start to tire of their boisterous behaviour. She is likely to begin sleeping on her own away from the kittens' bed. Once the kittens are at least eight weeks old, are fully weaned and are used to sleeping away from their mother, they can be moved to another home if this is the intention.

Caring for Orphaned Kittens

Rearing a whole litter of orphaned kittens is an extremely time-consuming task for the average owner, and if the situation occurs, by far the best solution is to find a good foster mother. Most cats will readily accept a few more kittens to nurse along with their own. However, if there are just one or two orphaned kittens and you really cannot find a foster mother, then it *is* possible (though difficult) to hand rear them.

Warmth is of major importance as they will not have the warmth of a mother's body to assist them. You will need to keep them in a room with a steady temperature of 30 degrees Centigrade (85 degrees Fahrenheit) at first, which can then be gradually lowered to 21 degrees Centigrade (70 degrees Fahrenheit) when they are six weeks old. It is quite a good idea to put a hot water bottle in a fleecy cover in their box and keep this constantly warm; they will snuggle up to this as a substitute mother. An infra-red lamp may also help with providing warmth.

A suitable milk substitute powder can be obtained from a vet. Cow's milk alone is inadequate because it does not contain enough protein to sustain proper growth. Special feeding bottles can also be obtained from your vet, but an eye-dropper will also make a good substitute provided that it has been thoroughly sterilised in boiling water. Give the freshly mixed milk powder to your kittens at a temperature of 38 degrees Centigrade (100 degrees Fahrenheit) and take it very slowly.

You must not rush the feeding process, otherwise your kittens may choke. They will probably only take a drop or two at a time. For the first two weeks they should be fed every two hours, for the second two weeks every four hours, and then every six hours after that until they are weaned.

To substitute for the way that their own mother would lick them, you should wipe over the kittens with a warm damp cloth after each meal and dry them thoroughly. This will encourage them to urinate and defecate, and the bedding will then need to be changed. It is vital to ensure that they are dried thoroughly, otherwise they may catch a chill.

If they become constipated, this can be corrected by adding

a few drops of liquid paraffin to the milk. Diarrhoea is more difficult to treat; try adding a small amount of cornflour to the milk, and if this does not quickly produce an improvement, consult your vet without delay. Diarrhoea in small animals can quickly lead to severe dehydration and this can be fatal.

A healthy kitten should double its birth weight at eight or nine days, and you should be able to introduce it to solid food after about three weeks. From then on you can proceed to treat it as if it were a normal kitten.

MATING PEDIGREE CATS

There is no real financial benefit to be gained from keeping and breeding from a pedigree queen, as far as the normal owner is concerned. It takes a specialist cat breeder years to establish a pedigree bloodline and this involves considerable effort and financial investment.

However, there are other good reasons for wanting to mate your cat within its own pedigree. Not everyone appreciates a cat which is 'cross-bred', i.e. a mixture of different varieties. You may prefer kittens which are pure-bred. Equally, if you are thinking of showing the kittens, then you may want to 'improve' on your cat's characteristics and produce a litter which is more technically 'perfect' according to the breed characteristics.

In these circumstances you would normally arrange to take your queen to a known breeder to be mated with a stud tom and pay the required stud fee for his services. If you do not already know a suitable breeder, then you can find one by looking at advertisements in cat magazines.

Before selecting a particular stud, it is well worth visiting a breeder's premises and getting to know them. The premises should be clean and well kept, with all the resident cats in good health. This is also a good time to discuss the fee, and any contractual conditions. The fee payable will depend on the status of the chosen stud tom and, as you would expect, you will have to pay more for a championship winner. There is usually no guarantee that kittens will be produced after a mating, although some breeders do offer a second mating free of charge if the first is unsuccessful.

Many breeders will also advise you on the selection of a suitable stud cat (a good stud tom should complement the strengths and weaknesses of your queen, so that a balance is achieved, rather than reinforcing your cat's faults and strong points). In theory the resulting kittens should then show an improvement on both parents.

Stud Procedure

It is general practice to mate a queen the second, rather than the first, time she comes into season, to ensure that her body is fully mature. A cat should really be at least eight months old before she has her first mating.

When your queen begins calling, you can make an appointment with the stud owner to take her in. Remember to take with you all the relevant documents such as your cat's pedigree and vaccination certificates, plus a diet sheet if she is a fussy eater. You must expect your cat to remain at the breeder's for several days while mating takes place.

When you arrive, do not be surprised if the breeder examines your queen for any signs of illness; it is in everyone's best interest to detect any symptoms of this and defer mating to a later date if necessary.

Mating quarters generally consist of two adjacent pens with a connecting door. The tom will already be installed in one of them and your queen will be released into the other to settle in, with the door between the two firmly shut at this stage. (Some queens can be quite wild at the smell of a tom in the vicinity.)

Once she has settled in, the queen will begin to show an interest in the other pen, usually by rubbing her body along the bars to attract the tom's attention. Once the breeder judges that the cats both want to mate and can mix safely, the connecting door will be opened and mating can then take place. The cats are normally separated after the mating, because the queen can become violent towards the tom afterwards. This procedure is then repeated on subsequent days, after which the queen can return home.

Once she has been mated, she should of course be kept indoors to ensure that she does not mate again and produce cross-bred kittens as a result.

Registration of Kittens

Pedigree kittens are normally registered at about six weeks old, once it is certain which sex they are. The procedure varies, depending on which breed they are and which association controls it. The purpose behind registration is to ensure that any member of a particular breed could be traced in the future, if necessary, and for this reason all cats must be given a unique name.

Most breeders have a prefix which they register for their own exclusive use and all kittens bred by them are then listed with this prefix, followed by another name. Pedigrees generally trace the parentage of a cat back through at least four generations. Advice on the naming of your particular cat should be sought from the breeder you are working with or from the relevant cat association.

7

COMMON CAT ILLNESSES AND HEALTH CARE

Cat illnesses are quite rare. If they are given a sensible diet, adequate exercise and regular inoculations, cats will seldom become ill. However, on the odd occasion that they do suffer illness, it is important to be able to recognise the symptoms and treat them appropriately.

The most obvious symptom of illness is a change in your cat's usual behaviour; if your normally active pet becomes listless and quiet, it is a good indication that there may be something wrong. Make sure that you keep your cat inside in the warmth with easy access to a litter tray and observe it closely over the next few hours.

If you have a veterinary thermometer and are able to check your cat's temperature yourself, then check to ensure that it has not risen above 38 degrees Centigrade (101 degrees Fahrenheit). (Even a rise of one per cent can indicate quite a severe illness.) If you are not able to check for yourself, then try to establish whether your cat has any other symptoms from the following list. This will help you to judge whether or not you need to consult a vet immediately.

LOSS OF APPETITE

If your cat is feeling unwell, then it may simply not want to eat. In this case it will probably just ignore its food bowl, and will turn its head away if you offer it a tasty piece of food by hand. If your cat is showing other symptoms as well, such as extreme listlessness, then you may want to consult your vet immediately, but if it is the only symptom you should wait until after the next usual mealtime. It is possible that your cat has overeaten and is just not hungry. Keep it indoors, and see whether its appetite returns within twenty-four hours. If not, consult your vet.

If however, your cat appears hungry and goes over to its food eagerly, but seems unable to eat it, then it may be suffering from a sore mouth. The problem could be a tooth, or a mouth ulcer. If the cat tries to eat, but is unable to swallow and regurgitates its food, then there is probably something stuck in its throat, and you will need to take it to the vet straightaway.

BLADDER PROBLEMS

Bladder problems are most often seen in females, who can suffer from the same type of cystitis infection as the one which commonly afflicts women. The symptoms you will observe will be the cat straining to pass a few drops of urine or blood. Unfortunately you will not be able to tell whether this is cystitis, or a more serious urinary infection (such as stones), because they both produce the same type of symptoms. If seen in the male cat, it is likely that these symptoms indicate a severe bladder complaint. In the case of both male and female cats you should consult your vet as soon as you see these symptoms, because they can develop into a very serious condition if left untreated. You should never give your cat dried food while it is suffering from this sort of problem, because it will only make the dehydration worse. Give moist food if the cat will eat it, and as much liquid as possible.

NOISY BREATHING

If your cat's breathing becomes laboured, or very noisy, you are seeing a real danger signal. Cats do not often have trouble breathing and this can indicate a serious condition such as a haemorrhage or pneumonia. It can also be caused by catarrh in the nasal passages, but in this case you should see signs of a runny nose as well. Take the cat to a vet immediately.

CONSTIPATION

If you observe your cat straining to pass its motions with little result, it is likely to be constipated. There may also be a dark brown discharge from the anus. Constipation can be caused by an unsatisfactory diet, although some cats are naturally more prone to it than others. Give the cat plenty of liquids and moist food, plus three teaspoons of liquid paraffin twice a day. You can try mixing the liquid paraffin with its normal food, but you may find that your cat refuses to touch it.

If this happens, obtain a small plastic syringe from your local pharmacy and squirt the liquid paraffin into the side of your cat's mouth. After twenty-four hours if there is no apparent relief or if the cat appears to be in pain, consult your vet. It is possible that the constipation may be a symptom of a more serious disorder such as a pelvic tumour.

DIARRHOEA

Diarrhoea must always be taken very seriously and treated straightaway. If it occurs in a kitten, see your vet immediately. In an adult cat, self-help may cure the problem unless it is very severe, but in a bad case always contact your vet for advice.

If it is not vomiting, the cat should be starved for twelve hours; if it is vomiting as well, the cat should be starved for twenty-four hours. By starving the cat, you are depriving the bacteria causing the diarrhoea of its food, because it lives and reproduces in the cat's stomach. You are also giving your cat a rest and a chance to start making a recovery.

On no account should you give your cat milk; in many cases the bacteria which cause diarrhoea thrive on milk, so this will make the problem worse. Water is preferable. If the anus appears very sore and painful, a small amount of petroleum jelly may be applied to the area to soothe it.

After this period of fasting, give your cat small quantities of food at a time, at fairly frequent intervals. Something light such as chicken or white fish would be ideal. If there are no apparent problems at this stage, then you can reintroduce the normal diet on the following day.

If, however, a fresh bout of diarrhoea begins when you reintroduce milk to the diet, you may have a cat who is allergic to cow's milk, so you will have to swap to goat's milk or a milk-free diet in future. Equally, if the problem recurs when you reintroduce a normal diet, consult your vet without delay.

MUSCULAR PAIN

If your cat suddenly yowls like mad when you touch it, the chances are that it is suffering from some kind of pain somewhere. The first thing to do if you observe this is to examine the cat very carefully from head to foot. You must be extremely gentle, to avoid hurting the cat any further. Look to see whether there is any obvious scratch or wound which could be the source of the pain. Infected wounds can be a great source of discomfort and they are not always easy to spot beneath a thick coat.

If there is no sign of a wound, check to see whether the cat can move all its limbs properly. If it is reluctant to use a leg, particularly if it avoids putting any weight on it and the limb appears to be stiff, then there is probably a sprained muscle there somewhere. This will generally improve by itself in a couple of days. If it will not put the leg on the floor at all, ask your vet to check it as soon as possible, because there may be a dislocation or a fracture to the bone which you cannot see.

INTERNAL PAIN

Internal pain is much harder to detect, but if you notice that your cat is purring constantly for no apparent reason and that it also seems reluctant to curl up, it may well have an abdominal problem. Look for tell-tale swelling and consult your vet for further advice.

VOMITING

Occasional vomiting is not too serious for most cats. It is really one of their bodies' mechanisms for getting rid of something undesirable from the stomach. Hairballs which build up in the stomach during grooming, worms or grass can all bring on an attack of vomiting. However, if vomiting becomes frequent or prolonged, then it can take a more serious turn and should be investigated. Since cats do not take in a lot of liquid, they can rapidly become dehydrated, so you should seek assistance from your vet in checking prolonged vomiting as soon as possible.

COMMON ILLNESSES

There are a number of illnesses which affect cats, the majority of which will require a proper diagnosis and treatment from your vet. However, it can be helpful to have some idea of what you are dealing with, so some of the most common ailments are listed here.

Abscess

Abscesses usually result from scratches or wounds inflicted by other cats, or sometimes even rats or foxes. They can occur anywhere on the skin or in the mouth, and will appear as a swelling with a shiny look to it, often very inflamed. Beneath the swelling is a collection of pus and the abscess may come to a 'head' and burst, oozing out foul-smelling matter. You may notice that your cat is showing signs of pain and keeps licking the affected area.

If the abscess has already burst by the time you notice it, then cut away the hair from the area and bathe it with warm water and a few drops of a suitable antiseptic such as Savlon or TCP. Continue bathing it at regular intervals until all the pus has been removed. You must not let it heal over while there is still pus present, otherwise a new abscess will form.

It is best to let your vet see the abscess as soon as you can, because the most effective treatment will be a course of antibiotics. In cases where the abscess has not burst on its own, the vet may also need to lance it.

Abscesses can also appear on a tooth, more usually in older cats. You will probably notice that your cat is reluctant to eat and appears to have a sore mouth. In this case the tooth will have to be taken out by a vet under anaesthetic.

Anaemia

Cats suffering from anaemia are very lethargic and have pale gums and tongues. This is a serious condition and can be due to many causes, including loss of blood, iron deficiency or Feline Infectious Anaemia. You should keep the cat warm and see your vet as soon as possible for advice.

Arthritis

Elderly cats may suffer from arthritis and have difficulty in walking and jumping, particularly after a long period of sleep. If you observe that your cat has become very stiff it may well be due to arthritis, but it is always best to check with your vet in case there has been an injury which you are not aware of.

Unfortunately there is no cure for arthritis, but the symptoms can be alleviated by keeping the cat out of the rain or damp conditions and ensuring that it has a warm, dry place to sleep in.

Bad Breath

This is an unusual symptom in cats, and one which you should not ignore. Always ask your vet for advice, because it can be caused by bad teeth, decaying food stuck between the teeth, a mouth ulcer or even a tumour.

Deafness and Ear Problems

Deafness can be a hereditary problem in some cats, notably the all-white cats with two blue eyes. Regrettably there is no treatment for this and the cat should not be allowed out unaccompanied, since it will not be able to hear the approach of vehicles on the road or indeed of any of its enemies. In old age, other cats may well develop deafness, which is also incurable.

However, deafness may also arise from other causes, for example from a build-up of ear wax. This condition is normally caused by the presence of ear mites, and can be successfully treated, if caught early enough.

Cats with ear mite infection will usually have a brown, waxy discharge in the ears and will be suffering from intense irritation. Generally they will scratch and shake their ears constantly in an effort to make them less itchy. Ear mites can be easily treated with ear drops from your vet, and the condition should soon clear up. If you have a dog, keep it away from the infected cat because ear mites can easily transfer to dogs.

An unfortunate complication of ear infections can be the 'puffy ear' syndrome. This is brought on by the cat's intense scratching and is usually caused by a burst blood vessel in the ear. The ear becomes inflamed and swollen, often looking as if it is filled with fluid, and will need to be lanced and drained by a vet.

Temporary deafness may also be caused by a bacterial infection in one or both ears, causing irritation and a foul-smelling discharge. It will need treating quickly with antibiotics, else it may spread to the inner ear and cause loss of balance. In severe cases the cat will hold its head to one side, and may wander round in circles before falling over.

Urgent veterinary attention is needed.

In some cases the cat may also develop small 'polyps' or wart-like growths in the ear canal. These can trap ear wax and obstruct the outer ear, often leading to a secondary bacterial infection and a smelly discharge. A vet will be able to remove the polyps under anaesthetic.

Eye Disorders

Eye disorders may occur on their own, but more often they will be present as symptoms of another infection such as cat 'flu. Cats can suffer from conjunctivitis which is an inflammation of the eye membrane, causing soreness and a reddening of the eye. There may also be a sticky discharge. You should bathe the affected eye with cool water which has previously been boiled, and then consult your vet for further advice.

You should also check to see whether there are any foreign bodies in the eyes, or if there are any scratches indicating that the cat has been fighting and may have received a blow to the eye. Gently bathe away anything you might find in the eye and give it a chance to recover. If there is no rapid improvement, then a trip to your vet is needed.

It is quite normal for the cat's third eyelid to come over the eyeball when there is any infection or irritation to the eye. This can look quite alarming and many owners have panicked when seeing it for the first time, thinking that their cat is going blind. The third eyelid is simply an additional protective membrane located in the corner of the eye. It can occasionally cover the eyeball when there is no obvious eye infection present, indicating that the cat is feeling unwell for some other reason. If this condition persists, consult your vet who may be able to diagnose some other cause.

Feline Enteritis Virus

This serious disease is a real killer, against which all cats should be annually vaccinated. It is passed on by contact with another infected cat and symptoms will develop four to ten days afterwards. Vomiting is usually the first symptom, followed by diarrhoea and a high temperature. The cat is usually thirsty and may suffer from abdominal pain.

If you suspect that your cat may be developing this disease, get treatment for it immediately from your vet. Although there is no specific drug which is effective against the virus, antibiotics may help to relieve the symptoms and give your pet a better chance of recovery.

Fleas

Fleas are the most common problem affecting cats today, and they can cause a great deal of irritation if left unchecked. They are a particular nuisance during the warm summer months, although if they are allowed to spread into a centrally-heated house they can survive to be a problem all year round. If your cat seems to be scratching a lot, especially around the neck region, fleas may well be the culprit. Look for tiny black flecks at the base of the cat's hairs; they appear like tiny particles of soot, but are actually flea droppings.

Once diagnosed, fleas can be easily treated with a good flea comb and any number of sprays or powders which are available on the market, or a good flea collar. You must also remember to destroy the cat's bedding, however, as this may be harbouring fleas or flea larvae. It is also worth vacuuming thoroughly in any areas of the house where the cat has been recently.

Hair Balls

This disorder is much more common in Long-Hairs than in Short-Hairs, and is generally worse during the moulting season. It is caused by loose hairs being swallowed during the grooming process, which then form a hard ball in the stomach. As a rule these are vomited up or passed in the faeces with no ill effect, but on occasion the hair remains wedged in the stomach which will then appear enlarged. Try giving the cat a teaspoon of liquid paraffin to induce the hair ball to pass out of the body normally. If this does not achieve the desired effect, then ask your vet for advice. Regular grooming by you will help to prevent the problem from recurring.

Incontinence
Unfortunately loss of control of the bladder and bowels is fairly common in elderly cats, and can be very upsetting both for them and for you. You should consult your vet for advice, but be prepared for the fact that there may not be a cure for this condition.

Influenza or Cat 'Flu
This is a very nasty disease, against which all cats should be regularly vaccinated. Some cats can act as 'carriers', showing no symptoms but infecting others, and it can spread extremely quickly.

The main symptoms are simular to 'flu in humans; sneezing, loss of appetite, coughing and a high temperature. Nasal discharge and an excessive production of saliva may follow. While the cat is ill, secondary infections can take place and cause other complications such as pneumonia which can be fatal. You should inform your vet immediately if you suspect that your pet has cat 'flu, and begin nursing it to make sure that it has the best possible chance of a good recovery.

Keep it somewhere warm and peaceful with everything it needs close at hand, especially plenty of fluids. Keep the nose and mouth free of discharge, wiping the cat's face regularly. Remember to make sure that you dry it properly afterwards. A cat is likely to feel very distressed if it cannot breathe and cannot keep itself clean, so assist it as much as you can. This will give it encouragement to fight the illness. Once it feels able to wash itself again it will be well on the road to recovery.

Kidney Disease
This is quite common in older cats and is characterised by thirst, loss of appetite and gradual weight loss. The cat may also develop bad breath, and vomit occasionally. These

symptoms are caused when the kidneys become unable to function properly, allowing impurities to build up in the cat's body. Although a full cure cannot usually be achieved, a trip to your vet is well worthwhile, because it may be possible to alleviate the symptoms and slow down the overall progress of the disease.

Lice

Like fleas, lice are a fairly common pest, but they are more usually found on cats in relatively poor condition. You will generally tell that a cat has lice because it will be scratching itself continually, and there may be bare, sore-looking patches on its skin.

If you examine the coat closely, it may appear to have dandruff, but this is in fact lice-eggs, or 'nits' as they are often called. The lice themselves cannot be seen easily with the naked eye. Lice are simply treated with special shampoos, powders or sprays and the condition should soon clear up. Many proprietary flea collars are also effective against lice.

Feline Leukaemia

Leukaemia is a blood disorder which does occur in cats quite frequently, although it is often hard to detect. It may give a wide variety of symptoms such as raised temperature, anaemia, thirst and mouth ulcers. If in doubt, consult your vet as soon as possible.

Pleurisy and Pneumonia

These are serious conditions affecting the lungs, often following on as a complication of cat 'flu. Both conditions can occur quite suddenly and will produce a rapid rise in temperature accompanied by distressed breathing. The cat will usually crouch and you will be able to see marked breathing movements. Loss of appetite is likely and the cat may also cry out in pain. You should get attention from a vet as fast as possible, so that antibiotics can give your cat a chance of recovery. Otherwise if these illnesses become acute they can be fatal.

Ringworm

Ringworm has nothing to do with worms; it is a fungal infection of the cat's skin, causing a rash of circular spots with a raised and sometimes crusty edge, red on the rim and pale in the middle. The spots will also glow in ultraviolet light. It is common in cats in poor condition, especially cats running wild in Mediterranean countries, and can spread very rapidly by body contact.

As this disease will spread with great rapidity over the cat's skin and it can also be passed on to humans, treatment should be obtained from your vet immediately. Avoid handling your cat if you suspect that it might have contracted ringworm, or use rubber gloves which you can then disinfect.

If any spots appear on your skin, see a doctor without delay for an ointment to cure them. All of the cat's bedding which might harbour the infection should be destroyed, and anything belonging to you should be put into a boil-wash and bleached if possible.

It takes weeks to eradicate ringworm completely, so any treatment which you have been given should still be applied to the affected area for a couple of weeks after the spots have disappeared. During this period, make sure that your cat is kept away from any other pets or children to whom it might pass on the infection.

Skin Mites ('Mange')

The group of skin diseases sometimes referred to as 'mange' is caused by various tiny mites which live on the skin or burrow into it, causing irritation and sometimes hair loss. If your cat is scratching a particular area constantly, or if you notice bald patches or spots, take the cat to a vet without delay. Mites can be treated quite easily, but the sooner the better, especially since your cat may otherwise create sores by scratching.

Remember to remove and burn your cat's bedding if it is diagnosed as having skin mites, and clean any other area where it has been recently. Otherwise it may risk becoming re-infected.

Ticks
Ticks are generally only a nuisance to cats living in country areas and they look like a sort of grey-blue shiny berry hanging on to the skin. Ticks feed off the cat's blood, and you should never attempt to pull them off, because part of them will be left under the skin and could cause a nasty infection.

Instead, smother the tick with surgical spirit or flea spray, which should cause it to release its hold and drop off within a few hours. If you then bathe the affected area with an antiseptic such as TCP it will heal naturally.

Tumours
Tumours are not necessarily 'malignant', (i.e. cancerous), many older cats suffer from tumours which are 'benign' (i.e. not harmful). They can occur in any part of the body or in the internal organs, so any lumps or bumps which are not obviously the result of a wound or an abscess should be shown to your vet.

The majority of tumours can be removed under anaesthetic, but it is important not to delay having this done, otherwise the tumour may grow and become harder to treat effectively.

Worms
There are two types of worm which commonly affect cats, roundworm and tapeworm. Many cats will carry these without showing any real signs of illness. Roundworms are brown-cream coloured, 8-10cm (3-4″) long, and are usually caught when the cat eats birds or rodents which are acting as a host to roundworm.

Tapeworms have long, segmented bodies and can cause a slight amount of disturbance to the cat's digestive system. The tapeworm passes out segments from the cat's anus which may stick to the hair around the tail region, looking like small grains of white rice. These may also be noticed on bedding. Tapeworms are passed on to the cat by swallowed fleas or small rodents, so double check that you are treating your cat properly for fleas, too. Both types of worm can cause irritation to the anal region and should be treated as soon as possible with worm tablets, or with a worming injection from your vet if your cat will not accept tablets. Bedding should also be destroyed and replaced.

It is vitally important to prevent children from handling an infected cat, and it is a good preventative measure to teach them always to keep their hands away from the cat's anal region, as well as washing their hands thoroughly after handling their pet. This will prevent any unfortunate cross-infection if they handle an infected cat and put their hands in their mouths afterwards.

As a general rule, it is far better to ensure that your cat does not become a source of infection in the first place by dosing it regularly with worm tablets. Prevention is much better than cure.

INJURIES AND ACCIDENTS

If you know that your cat has been involved in an accident, especially a car accident, make sure that you take it to the vet for a check-up, even if it appears unharmed. It may have sustained internal injuries which are undetectable except to the trained eye.

If the cat is obviously injured, check that it can breathe properly and that there is nothing obstructing the passage of air (e.g. its tongue or anything else stuck in the throat). Prepare a suitable cat carrier and then pick up the cat by the scruff of the neck, supporting the body with your other hand, and lay it in the carrier, preferably with a cover over it to keep it warm. Get veterinary attention for it as soon as possible.

Fig. 23.   How to hold an injured cat;
the 'scruff' must be grasped very firmly.

Bleeding

If heavy bleeding occurs, try to stop the flow by applying a pad of cotton wool or clean cloth soaked in water and squeezed out. Apply firm pressure and take the cat to a vet as fast as possible.

If the blood is spurting out from a leg or foot, then you will need to apply a tourniquet, otherwise the cat may bleed to death before you get assistance. You will need a piece of cord or something similar such as a man's tie or a lady's stocking. Tie it around the injured limb as tightly as you can possibly manage, between the point of blood loss and the heart. Keep it like this for two minutes, which should stop the spurting.

You *must* loosen it a little after two minutes, and then after eight minutes you should take it off again to allow some circulation, even if it starts to bleed heavily again. It is dangerous to cut off the circulation for any longer than a few minutes; you risk the eventual loss of the limb. It is vital to seek professional help as quickly as possible.

Burns and Scalds

The old saying 'curiosity killed the cat' is based on a lot of truth; cats are extremely inquisitive animals. Sadly, this often leads them into trouble, and many of them do get injured as a result. Be aware that open fires, burning rubbish, hot bonfire ashes, and most importantly hot ovens, electric cooker rings and gas jets are all hazardous to your cat. Equally, panfuls of boiling water or hot kettles are just as likely to cause injury. Do try to keep your cat well away from these sources of danger.

If the worst happens and your cat does get burned or scalded, and the skin is not broken, treat the injured paw or limb as you would your own and hold it under running cold water for five minutes if you can. Then take the cat to the vet for advice and proper treatment.

Choking

This usually happens when something gets stuck in the cat's throat, such as a piece of bone. You should immediately open the cat's mouth and try to see what is causing the problem, removing it if possible. Try using tweezers if the object is hard to grasp. If you cannot see anything, hold the cat upside down, grasping it firmly by the hind legs, and give it a sharp tap between the shoulders. This may dislodge a foreign body stuck in the throat.

If you are still unable to get to the cause of the problem, take the cat to a vet without delay as severe choking can lead to lack of oxygen and eventual death.

Drowning

Although most cats can swim if they need to, it is possible that they could become exhausted and drown if they are unable to get out of the water they have fallen into; in this case you need to act quickly after you have rescued them. The first thing to do is to clear the air passages and lungs. Speed is vitally important.

Check that there is nothing obstructing the cat's breathing and that the nose, mouth and throat are clear. Next, pick up the cat by its hind legs with the head pointing downwards and swing it gently round in a circle. This should drain any water from its lungs. If it is not breathing, then you will need to give it artificial respiration. (Even if the cat appears to be dead, it may breathe again after resuscitation, so it is always worth a try.)

Place the cat on its side, open its mouth and make sure that the tongue is pushed down to the bottom of the mouth where it cannot block the air flow. Press down firmly on the rib cage with the palm of your hand, count to four and then release. (This will stimulate the lungs into working normally.) Repeat this twice and normal breathing may return. If it does not, then you can try mouth-to-mouth resuscitation.

Put one hand over the cat's nostrils and cup your other hand around the cat's mouth. Take a deep breath and blow into the cat's mouth to inflate the lungs. Take another breath and repeat. If this technique is successful, then the cat will start to breathe on its own again. If after trying for ten minutes or so there is no response, then unfortunately the cat is dead and cannot be revived.

Eyes

If there has been a severe blow to the eye, then it may have been partially knocked out of its socket. This is a surprisingly common injury in cats, and is often caused by a road accident or by cat fights. It is usually possible to put the eye back into its socket under anaesthetic, provided that it has not been too badly damaged, so take the cat to a vet without delay. Even if it has been too badly damaged to be restored, do not despair; a cat will learn to manage quite successfully with only one eye.

Fish Hooks

Injuries from fish hooks are most common in country areas, or in places where there is access to a canal, river or lake. Occasionally a hook will become caught in the cat's mouth.

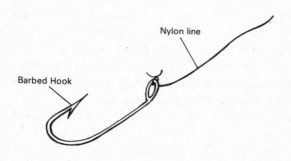

Fig. 24. A fish hook.

Never try to pull the hook straight out; most fishing hooks are barbed and you will do more harm than good. It is best to take your cat straight to a vet who will be able to remove the hook under anaesthetic with the minimum of fuss and the least possible damage to the cat's mouth.

Paint, Oil and Tar

You should always keep your cat away from any fresh paint or similar, particularly if it is on skirting boards or doors as these are exactly the places where a cat will normally rub its body. If it does have the misfortune to get any of these substances on its fur, you will need to act quickly before it tries to clean itself and makes the problem worse by swallowing the contaminant as well. In severe cases it is best to go directly to your vet for assistance, but for small amounts you can probably treat the problem at home.

Paint

If it is water-based, such as emulsion, then sponge the area with water until the fur becomes clean again. For other paints such as gloss, you will probably need to use a nailbrush and a solution of washing up liquid and warm water, or a skin cleaner such as Swarfega. Do not use turpentine, white spirit or brush cleaner on your cat's skin because these will sting and cause an irritation, as well as being poisonous if the cat licks them. If there are large amounts of paint matted into the coat, then it may be easiest to clip off the affected fur, especially if the cat is a Long-Hair.

Oil/Tar

Clean as much of the excess off the coat as you can, using paper towelling. Then follow the process for gloss-paint given above. In addition, your vet may be able to supply a tar-remover if you are unsuccessful with Swarfega or washing-up liquid solution.

Poisoning

Cats are much less susceptible to poisoning than dogs, being naturally very careful about what they eat; however, it *can* happen. If you suspect that your cat has eaten something poisonous, try to make it sick by tilting its head back and tipping an egg-cupful of salty water into its mouth. With luck it may then vomit up whatever it has swallowed. If you have the empty container then take it with you to the vet, so that the substance can be identified if possible.

Even if you are not aware of any poisons in or around your home, it is possible that your cat may have come into contact with one elsewhere. The usual symptoms are very excitable behaviour, staggering and possible diarrhoea and vomiting. You should take the cat to a vet immediately.

Cats Stuck in Trees

Cats are born climbers, and will often climb into very high trees from curiosity, or from a desire to catch an elusive bird. They will also sometimes use them as a means to escape from a threat on the ground. However, as they find it easier to climb upwards than they do to descend down a slippery tree-trunk, they can on occasions get stuck.

In most cases, it is simply a lack of confidence which prevents a cat from coming down again; they do not often get physically stuck between the branches. As a general rule, if left in peace they will come down in a day or so, when they get hungry enough.

The worst thing that you can do is to try to climb up after them; this can startle cats and make them climb even higher into the tree. If however, there is no sign of them coming down after a day or so, then you might want to try putting a ladder up the tree on the opposite side to the way you want the cat to come down, and starting to climb up it. The cat will probably be frightened by the ladder and will take the obvious escape route down to the ground.

If the tree is very high and the cat shows no sign of coming down after two days, then you can try calling the Fire Brigade, but they will normally only come out to rescue a cat if it is physically stuck in the tree and cannot come down of its own accord. Obviously it is a waste of their time to turn up with a team of men and expensive equipment, only to find that the terrified cat runs down the tree all by itself as soon as it sees them.

Wounds and Cuts

You should only attempt to deal with slight wounds and cuts yourself, as cats' wounds do have a tendency to get infected easily. Any deep wounds should be dealt with by your vet, rather than you. For a slight cut, though, there is no problem with treating it at home.

First you should bathe the wound with cotton wool soaked in a mild antiseptic solution, such as TCP, to clean out any dirt or grit from it. It may be a good idea to clip away any hair from the surrounding area, too. Then cover the wound with a piece of sterile gauze or a dressing made for this purpose (sterile wound dressings are available in packs from any pharmacy) and hold it firmly in place with adhesive tape. Change the dressing on a daily basis until the wound has healed.

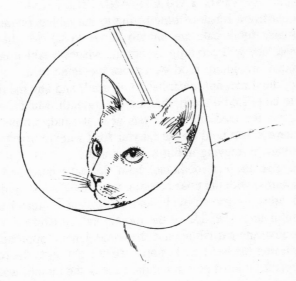

Fig. 25.   An Elizabethan collar.

If the cat shows a tendency to keep removing the dressing and the wound is too deep to be left to heal in the fresh air, then you may need to put an Elizabethan collar on your cat to prevent it from picking at the dressing. You can either take your cat to your vet to have the wound professionally dressed and a collar applied (vets will supply a ready-made collar and it is probably a good idea to let them see the wound anyway while you are there), or you can make one at home.

It can be made from a piece of thin cardboard or very stiff paper, shaped into a funnel. This is attached around the cat's neck, preventing it from licking or chewing any dressing on its body. The collar can be simply fastened with sellotape, once you have got the size correct and have placed it around the cat's neck.

GIVING TABLETS AND MEDICINE

It is usually a waste of time trying to put tablets or medicine in a cat's food; cats are far too clever to fall for that ruse. Instead they will carefully eat around whatever tablet has been included, or ignore food which has medicine in it.

So, the direct approach has to be used, and any medication has to be placed directly into the cat's mouth. Make sure that you have the medicine or tablets near at hand, because once you have a firm hold on the cat you don't want to have to upset it further by moving about unnecessarily.

To give the cat medicine, hold the cat's head and tilt it backwards, with the nose pointing upwards. This should cause it to open its mouth wide and allow you to manoeuvre a spoonful in to the side of the mouth and tip it in.

To give the cat tablets use the same general approach, but after tilting the head back, pop a tablet right on to the back of the tongue. It must be right at the back of the mouth, well over the bridge of the tongue where there are very few taste-buds. If you get this position absolutely correct, then the tablet will be immediately swallowed. You will see the cat licking its lips, which is confirmation that it has swallowed it.

If you do not get the position exactly right, then the cat will spit the tablet out and will probably run off. If it has tasted a bitter tablet, it may also produce large amounts of saliva. This can look rather worrying, but it is quite a normal reaction and so it is no real cause for concern. It is easiest to give the cat a few minutes to recover from the experience and then try again.

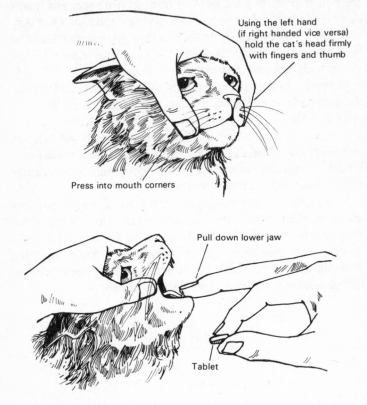

Using the left hand (if right handed vice versa) hold the cat's head firmly with fingers and thumb

Press into mouth corners

Pull down lower jaw

Tablet

Fig. 26.   Giving tablets.
             Above: Restraining the head.
             Below: Administering the tablet; maintain
                    pressure on the mouth corners.

After the cat has swallowed the tablet, or medicine, you may like to give it a small piece of fish or chicken to take away any aftertaste.

CONVALESCENCE, OLD AGE AND EUTHANASIA

As you can see from the above, with prompt treatment and care and attention during illness, most cats will make a good recovery. The attention in itself seems to be beneficial; cats seem to respond to good nursing from their owners and it acts as a morale booster for them. This is very important when they are feeling ill, especially if they cannot get out and about to keep themselves properly clean. Without this attention they can quickly become depressed and deteriorate.

However, as they get older, they can sometimes suffer from the incurable troubles of old age which can make life very wretched for them and for you (e.g. arthritis, kidney failure, loss of bowel control). If this happens, and your vet believes that their condition cannot be improved, it may perhaps be kinder to consider euthanasia than to leave them to deteriorate slowly and suffer a lingering death.

Euthanasia is generally performed by a single painless injection after which the cat will slide into a deep sleep followed by death after the heart stops beating. It is over quickly and peacefully. It is obviously a very upsetting decision to have to make, but it is much more merciful than letting your pet suffer a slow, painful illness.

8

CATS ON THE MOVE

TRAVEL AND YOUR CAT

In order to make travel as stress-free as possible, you should start getting your cat used to its basket or cat carrier at an early age. Repetition will make the whole experience familiar and therefore much less frightening. You should practise by putting the cat in the cat basket, moving it about, then letting the cat out again. Remember to include some bedding or a towel to line the basket; it will smell like home and will help the cat to accept being carried. Once the cat has got used to the basket, you may like to try a few short trips in the car, so that your pet treats this as a routine occurrence. You will then be able to transport your cat safely, with the minimum of distress caused to it and to you.

Preparing your Cat for its Journey

It is sensible to allow your cat as much freedom to run around and exercise as possible, before confining it in a basket for any length of time. This will also give it the opportunity to work off excess energy and may make it sleepy enough to doze for some of the time.

If the journey is a long one, it is best to feed the cat several hours before the expected journey time. This will then give it the opportunity to digest its food, run around and go outside or use a litter tray, as necessary. This will minimise the risk of any accidents in transit. (However, it is also a good idea to line the cat basket with polythene under the blanket or towel, just in case.)

Most cats will not allow themselves to be confined in a

basket from choice, so even if you have managed to train them to accept being carried in the basket, it is probably best to keep it out of sight while you are feeding them. Otherwise, they may disappear off when you let them out and delay your journey. If the journey is a short one, you may find it easier to call the cat in at a normal mealtime and arrange for it to be fed at its destination.

Accompanied Travel by Road, Sea, Air or Train
It is always best to accompany your cat if at all possible, because your presence will have a calming effect on it during what is essentially a very frightening experience. There will be many strange sights, sounds and smells which will confuse and disorientate the cat and it will be far happier if it has the reassurance of having its owner with it. Also, you will be able to supervise its journey and ensure that it is taken care of properly.

If you are travelling by train or coach, then you will be able to keep the cat with you at all times. This usually also applies if you are travelling by ferry. If you are travelling by air, however, you will not be able to keep the cat with you. It will need to be checked in as baggage and will be individually handled. (Only guidedogs are allowed in passenger cabins.) It is best to consult the individual airlines for their guidelines on this before you travel, and you should make sure that your cat's travelling basket is well labelled.

Travelling Unaccompanied
If it is impossible to accompany your cat, then the next best thing is to take it to wherever its journey will begin yourself, and arrange for someone to meet it at its destination. You should inform the carriers about this beforehand, and make sure that the cat carrier is labelled with the name and address of the person meeting it as well as the required destination.

If it is not possible to arrange for someone to collect it, then there are a number of specialist transport companies who would be pleased to arrange the travel for you. They will also provide a suitable cat carrier and advise you about the travel regulations. Cats are classified as livestock, so there are strict rules governing how they may be transported.

Taking your Cat Abroad

If you are planning to take your cat out of the U.K., then you will need to carry with you a certificate guaranteeing its health and fitness. A vet will be able to provide you with this, and you should arrange for your cat to be seen shortly before you are due to travel, so that the certificate is up to date. Most countries also require a certificate to say that your cat has been vaccinated against rabies, so it is a good idea to have your cat inoculated at the same time.

Britain is in general far more strict about quarantine rules than most other countries, and does not recognise the rabies vaccination as sufficient in itself to protect against the disease. You will find that the majority of other countries will happily admit a British cat holding a rabies inoculation certificate with no further fuss at all. However, one or two countries may insist on a short period of quarantine immediately after arrival. It is best to check what the rules are well in advance of your trip, so that the appropriate arrangements may be made in good time.

British Quarantine Regulations

Because Britain is a rabies-free country, the quarantine regulations are deliberately very stringent, to make sure that we keep it that way. Rabies is not only a vicious disease which causes tremendous suffering and finally death to animals, it can also infect and kill people. The period between original infection and the appearance of the first symptoms of the disease can be anything up to six months, which explains why it is so hard to track down carriers and eradicate the disease, once it is present. Britain is one of the few countries which have managed to get rid of it, helped by the fact that it is an island and has stringent customs controls.

Because the incubation period for rabies is so long, and an apparently healthy animal may become ill several months after arriving at our shores, the British quarantine period has to be six months. Quarantine involves the cat being kept in an isolation pen, in a boarding cattery which is recognised as being suitable for quarantine purposes. Such a cattery will be authorised by the Government, and in general there will only be one in any given area. There may not be another within a fifty mile radius.

For this reason, planning and booking in advance is vitally important if you are intending to bring a cat in to the U.K. British cats may, of course, be moved freely between U.K. countries with no restrictions; this includes Wales, Scotland, England, Northern Ireland, the Republic of Ireland, the Isle of Man and the Channel Islands.

If you are going to bring a cat into the U.K. from abroad, then you will need to obtain a licence to do so. Without this, the cat will not be allowed on British land. Licences can be obtained from the Ministry of Agriculture, Fisheries and Food (address in the Appendix).

The licences will stipulate that any imported animal must be transported from the point of entry into the U.K. to a Government Authorised Quarantine Premises by authorised carrying agents. A list of these approved agents can be obtained from the Ministry. The animal will then have to be kept isolated from other animals for six months, and vaccinated twice during this period with an approved anti-rabies vaccine. After the six months' quarantine it is certified rabies-free and may travel freely within the U.K.

MOVING HOUSE

Moving house can be a difficult time for all of us, but for a cat it is even more traumatic, because cats are so territorial. Even a change in furnishings will be upsetting to a cat, so the inevitable disruption which accompanies a house move is very hard for it to cope with. Add to that the fact that its owners will be tense and tired, and you can see that it is a very distressing time altogether.

Preparing for the Move

Fortunately there are a few simple measures which you can take to limit the extent to which your cat is upset by all the packing and disruption which go on before a house move. The first is to allow it as much time outside as possible; the garden and surrounding area will be reassuringly familiar and unchanged, and the cat will be out from under your feet. You can then take on any noisy packing of crates and moving of smaller items without the added hassle of a cat touring round miaowing at you.

If possible, try to pile up full crates in one room and close the door to it, before allowing the cat back in. If you can keep most of the rooms in your house looking relatively normal, then your cat will cope far better than it will if every single room has piles of boxes and rearranged furniture in it. Above all, hide any sign of suitcases being packed, otherwise the cat may come to the conclusion that you are going away on holiday and may believe it is due for a trip to the cattery. This is never beneficial for its health and temper.

Make sure that you have stocked up on food and cat litter, because you will need them on moving day and probably for a few days afterwards while your cat is settling in to its new home. Collect all the cat's things together and keep them somewhere which is easily accessible; you don't want suddenly to find that the litter tray is at the bottom of any one of twenty-five fully-packed crates just when you need it.

If you can, try to empty one room completely and put all the cat's things in there, including its litter tray. You will then be able to shut the cat inside while the removal men pack up the rest of your belongings and it will be safe until you collect it.

On Moving Day

If the cat has been let out the night before, then it will have had plenty of opportunity to run around and exercise, so there will be no problem with keeping it indoors for a few hours. It is best to feed it and then shut it inside one room, preferably one which removal men have no cause to go into. It is a good idea to label the door with a notice saying 'Please do not open, scared cat inside'. This should prevent them from opening the door to check what is inside and allowing the cat to bolt out and possibly escape through the open front door. All the noise of moving and the strangers in the house would be enough to make the cat disappear for a good few hours, which could cause you a real problem if it is allowed to escape outside.

If your cat does not normally go outside at night, then you can let it out for an hour or so while you are having breakfast if you feel that it should have some exercise, but in this case do not feed it before you let it go outside. If it is hungry, it will return back to be fed once it has had a short run, and you can then confine it in one room while the furniture and crates are packed in the van.

If you make sure that food, water and a litter tray are all in the room with the cat, it should survive quite happily in there for several hours, which should be ample time to pack the contents of the house. It is also a good idea to have the cat basket in there too, so that you aren't hunting for it when the time comes to move the cat. A couple of plastic carrier bags would also be useful to keep at hand (although not in the room with the cat in, in case it gets inside one and suffocates) so that you can pack up the litter tray and food dishes easily to transport them to your new home.

Finally, once everything else has been packed and the removal van is ready to leave, you can pack up the cat's dishes and litter tray, and place the cat in the cat basket. The cat can then travel with you to the new house. Remember to bring with you the notice from the door; you will need this again later.

Arriving at the New House

When you arrive at your new home, you will need to select another room which you can keep empty and in which you can safely keep the cat for the next few hours, during the unloading process. It doesn't have to be a particularly big room, in fact a small one may well be better, because the cat will get to know it faster. Remember that at first it will smell new and frightening to an already bewildered cat. So, a small, fairly empty room such as a bathroom or cloakroom is ideal.

Put the cat inside it, still in its basket, and unpack its food and water dishes and litter tray. Then open the door or lid of the cat basket, and leave the cat to come out on its own once it feels happy to do so. Leave it in the room to settle down, and remember to put your warning notice on the outside of the door, so that everyone knows that the cat is now in there and the door should remain shut.

Once the removal men have gone and you have walked around the house making sure that all the doors and windows are firmly closed (and any cat-flap is secured) you can let your cat out to begin exploring its new home. If you have been able to organise a room to sit down in, such as the living room, then it is probably best to take the cat in here to start with.

It will be familiar with the smell of your sofa, chairs and similar furniture and this will help it to settle down. You will probably find that it seems very nervous at first, but it will soon increase in confidence as it begins to learn its way around. All the same, you should ignore any pleas to go outside at this stage, because your cat will not have fully settled down yet.

Be very careful for the first few hours when you open doors or windows; make sure that you know exactly where the cat is and shut it in. Otherwise it may make a sudden dash for freedom and become lost before it has had a chance to reorientate itself.

Once your cat has begun to learn its way around the new house, you can establish where you are going to feed it in future. You should move its bed, food dishes and litter tray to the new location and show your cat where they are. It will then be able to work out its routes around the house and back to its home base.

If your cat suddenly disappears in the first few hours of exploration, do not be unduly alarmed. It has probably found somewhere safe to hide until it can come to terms with the new surroundings. It may have hidden somewhere high, such as on top of a cupboard or wardrobe, or somewhere enclosed such as underneath a bed or in a corner behind a heavy piece of furniture.

It will come out again when it is ready, and coaxing it is not likely to make much difference. Leave it to settle in its own time. If it is left in peace it is likely to readjust to its new home much faster than if you spend ages calling it and trying to entice it out. However, it *is* worth doing a quick check around the house and opening cupboard doors, to make sure that it hasn't been shut inside accidentally during the unpacking.

Going Outside

Once you are sure that your cat is thoroughly familiar with its new house, you can think about letting it go outside to explore further. Do be certain that your cat is showing no signs of distress before attempting this; it should be eating properly and should not appear nervous or unsure of itself and its surroundings. (You are likely to have to wait at least a couple of days after moving, although cats vary and some will settle within a day or so.) It is better to be safe than sorry though, so wait until you are sure. Remember to change your address inside the cat's tag if it has one, just in case it gets itself lost, or its curiosity entices it into a neighbour's garage and it gets locked in.

It is best to begin by letting your cat explore the back garden first, because it is enclosed and safer. The cat can progress to the front door in its own time, once it has learned its way around. It is preferable to let your cat out in daylight hours to begin with, so that you can be certain that it knows the location before you allow it out after dark. It can be a good idea to let it out shortly before a mealtime, so that it won't feel keen to stray too far from home.

You will probably find that the cat stays fairly close to the house door to begin with, and may keep coming back to it to check its bearings. It may also keep coming in and out of the door, which may seem irritating to you, but it is really only the cat's way of checking its route back to base. Fortunately this phase does not usually last long.

Once outside, the cat will probably spend a lot of time sniffing, and marking the new territory by rubbing its body against key places such as walls and fences. This is all part of the familiarisation process. After an hour or so your cat will have learned the new territory and may very well launch itself over the nearest fence to explore further. Don't panic; it will very soon be back again to check its route to the door.

Once your cat has satisfactorily been out and returned home a couple of times with no problems, it is safe to start letting it out at night. Remember to check that the new house has some shelter available for your cat; this can be in a garage, a garden shed or through a cat-flap into the house itself.

9

COPING WITH HOLIDAYS
AND PARTIES

Holidays and parties are fantastic fun for you and your family, but sadly they are not always so much fun for your cat. Cats loathe disruption, noise and crowds of people. They also hate change to their home surroundings, and they intensely dislike having to leave their home base. So, the necessary preparations for any holiday, party or even a weekend away must involve some planning on behalf of your cat, too, so that it doesn't have to suffer while you enjoy yourself.

WEEKENDS AWAY

If you are planning to go away for the weekend, then you will need to consider the various options for taking care of your cat during your absence. As cats hate to leave their home territory and a weekend is really quite a short period of time, probably the best solution is to arrange for someone to come in and look after your cat for you. This will only work well if it is someone who the cat knows and is used to seeing regularly. It will also have to be someone reliable, who will arrive at the right time when your cat is expecting to be fed, and who is willing to take on the chore of emptying the litter tray if the cat is being kept inside the house.

It is really best to continue to allow your cat to go outside if that is what it is used to, but that may involve your 'cat-sitter' in spending quite some time at your house. If your cat is the sort who disappears off for hours at a time, it may be best to let it 'live' in the garage or shed for the weekend if the weather is reasonable, and arrange for your cat-sitter to put its food and drink in there. Otherwise they might well end up waiting at your house for a very long time indeed, and may refuse ever to cat-sit again!

This approach would work quite well if your cat is used to sheltering in the shed or the garage under normal circumstances. Even if it is not, you can still use this method of feeding your cat, but you should take it to the new location and show it that you have put its bed and feeding bowls in there before you leave. This way it will be sure to go straight there when it gets hungry.

Failing the possibility of a cat-sitter, you can still use a similar solution and leave enough food and drink for your cat's requirements in the house, or in the shed or garage. Pet shops sell a gadget known as an automatic feeder, which is basically two large lidded cat bowls with a 48-hour timer on each, powered by a battery. They are kept cold by a pack of the same type of coolant which is normally used in a coolbox; you put it into the freezer or fridge freezer compartment overnight before placing it underneath the bowls, and it will then ensure that the food remains fresh.

The individual bowls will each hold a day's ration of food, and can be set so that the lids pop open at your cat's normal mealtime. These automatic feeders are initially quite expensive to buy, but they are sturdy and will last for many years once purchased. If you often go away for weekends it may well be worth the investment of buying one. (If your local pet shop does not stock them, contact Pets Pleasure who offer a catalogue mail order service. Their address is given in the Appendix.)

The third option if you are going away is of course to board your cat at a suitable cattery, although for a short period such as a weekend your cat would probably prefer to be at home. As a cat will take a day or so to settle anywhere new, it will not have had time to get used to being at the cattery before you collect it again. It will therefore have had a very unsettled few days.

Of course, the benefits of boarding are that you can be certain that if you have chosen a good cattery, your cat will be getting excellent care all the time that you are away. If your cat is old, recovering from an illness, or is a fairly new kitten, then of course a cattery is much the best option to choose if you are going away.

THE ANNUAL HOLIDAY

When you are planning your annual break from home, remember the cat. You will need to make arrangements for it to have its own holiday at a good boarding cattery, and if you are planning to be away during the school holidays, do make sure that you book early.

Allow plenty of time either side of flight or other travel times, to make sure that you are not rushing to take the cat in, or to collect it after your holiday has ended. If the schedule is tight, then book an extra day rather than have a mad panic to get there on time. Remember that flights are often delayed, so allow a couple of extra hours for this and always take the telephone number of the cattery with you when you travel. This way you will be able to contact them immediately if there is a change of plan.

You should also check that your cat has been vaccinated against feline enteritis and cat 'flu recently, and that it will still be covered at the time it is going to be boarding. All good catteries will ask for proof of inoculation before accepting your cat for boarding, and you really don't want to find out at the last minute that your cat's booster is overdue.

Selecting a Boarding Cattery

As with many things in life, the best way of finding a good boarding cattery in your area is by personal recommendation. Ask your friends with cats which one they use and what they think of it, or try asking your vet. Failing that, you will have to search through the local directory to see what is available in your area.

In any case, there is no substitute for visiting any selected cattery and having a good look around yourself. I would always advise turning up unannounced during normal working hours; that will give you the opportunity to make an inspection of the premises in their normal state. If you explain politely that you are planning to board your cat in the near future and are very fussy about where you take it, so can you please have a chat and a look around, most cattery owners will be more than happy to let you look over the premises.

Doing this will also give you the chance to have a discussion with them and form an impression of the cattery as a whole. Be very suspicious if an owner appears reluctant to let you see the cat pens or asks you to come back at a later time; they may well have something to hide. It is probably best to avoid that cattery and look elsewhere.

When you look around the cattery, check that it all looks and smells clean and fresh. The pens should be warm (but not too stuffy) and everywhere should be nice and dry. If there are a number of cats in at the time you make your visit, that is quite a good sign; it proves that the business is thriving. Have a look at how the cats seem; if they appear healthy and reasonably contented and they all have clean litter trays and full water dishes, then all is as it should be. Seeing a pile of dirty food dishes or litter trays which have not been cleaned out is a bad sign, although if you have arrived in the morning just after feeding time, then you must give the staff the benefit of the doubt.

The pens themselves should be quite large and spacious, preferably on a split level with a scratching log and a couple of shelves for the cat to sit on. They should appear secure and well-maintained. If they are located outside and you are planning to board your cat during the winter months, look for some means of heating. If you cannot see any, then ask. It is also worth asking how the cats are normally fed, and whether this will accommodate your cat's usual diet. Also check whether there is a vet on call if necessary. If all the answers to these questions are favourable and you feel that you would be happy to trust the cattery owner with your pet, then you have found the perfect cattery.

Returning Home After Boarding

Most cats are absolutely delighted to be returning home after a stay at the boarding cattery, however good it is. The simple fact of being able to wander around the house at will again, after being confined in a pen for so long, is extremely welcome. Although they will be back on home territory, it can take a while for them to readjust to the usual routine, and you will find that it takes a little time for them to get back to normal.

The first symptom of this which you can expect to see is that cats will tour round their territory, exploring every room in the house. After they have spent half an hour or so doing this, it is probably a good idea to feed them, so that they are reminded that this is home and they will settle down more quickly.

Keeping them in for the first night is a good idea, and should be quite acceptable as they have been using a litter tray at the cattery anyway. This is especially true if you have boarded them for more than a week and you return in the late afternoon or evening; in this case there has not been adequate time for them to settle back in at home and they may still be confused. By the next evening they should be back to normal and it will be perfectly safe to let them out again.

BONFIRE NIGHT

The shooting rockets, sudden sparks and crackling bonfires which are so exciting to us can spell fear and disaster to a cat if it is not protected. All the strange shrieks, bangs and hisses can be terrifying, and a cat which is out after dark risks getting singed, or even blinded, if it is unlucky enough to be in just the wrong place at the wrong time.

The only real way to keep your cat safe and happy during Bonfire Night is to keep it inside all night. This precaution also needs to be extended to the other nights during the first week of November, as well as the two weekends either side of Bonfire Night itself, because people may well choose to hold parties on nights other than November 5th. Of course if your cat is in the habit of going out, you will need to provide it with a litter tray indoors for use during Bonfire week and show it where this is located, so that it can use it when necessary. If you forget this, you will probably have to deal with a very unhappy cat yowling by the door in distress.

The first time that your new pet experiences Bonfire Night it is really best to stay indoors with it if you can, because you can then assess how well it is coping with all the noise and disturbance. Your presence will also be very reassuring for the cat, and will help it to cope.

Some cats are much more nervous than others and can be very upset indeed by shrieking fireworks and flashes of light across the sky; others will take it more or less in their stride, provided that they are safe inside a warm, familiar environment. Quite often they will find somewhere to hide which feels particularly secure, such as right underneath a bed, and will stay there until all the noise is over. It can help a great deal to leave lights on in the house, because this will lessen the impact of sudden flashes of strange-coloured lights from fireworks lighting up the sky. Even if your cat has been through several Bonfire Nights with very little apparent distress, it is still worth leaving a light on, especially if you are planning to go out and leave it in the house. Do draw all the curtains, too, to reduce the impact of lights outside.

If you find that your cat becomes very nervous and upset, try soothing it on your knee and putting on some background noise such as the television, radio or CD player which will help to distract it. It may still decide to bolt upstairs and hide, though, in which case the best thing to do is to let it stay wherever it feels most secure.

CHRISTMAS

Christmas is a marvellous time of the year, but it can be an upsetting one for a pet, because of all the noise and excitement and the vast numbers of extra people coming to the house to visit, or even to stay there. Furniture is often moved around, a huge tree arrives in the house, decorations and cards go up and everyone is rushing about like mad. To a cat who loves peace and tranquility, this is not an ideal time, particularly if your house is one where there are excited young children as well.

To help your cat to cope with this stressful time of the year, try to keep some rooms of the house quiet and unchanged, so that the cat can seek a refuge in there. Do persuade any children to allow it a little peace and quiet and time to itself, undisturbed. You may find that it exercises its own choice in this and spends a lot of time outside, but it may be rather cold at this time of year so a quiet room is really best.

Do make sure that you keep your cat out of the kitchen during preparations for Christmas dinner; the aroma of a huge turkey cooking will tantalise even the most well-behaved cat into trying to snatch a piece, and at the very least it will be constantly under your feet begging. It is far better to make the kitchen out of bounds.

It goes without saying that Christmas is *not* the time to acquire a new cat as a pet, or as a present for one of the family. It is a very bad time to try to settle a new, bewildered animal into a household, and you will not be able to devote enough time to its needs. No-one wants to have to deal with a terrified, miaowing cat which might be soiling its bedding and possibly the carpet as well, in the midst of all the festivities. This will be a very bad start for the cat and for you, and it is the sort of mistake which leads to so many poor

cats and kittens being abandoned over the Christmas period
and ending up in cat refuges.

If you *must* give a cat as a Christmas present, then do it
by giving a card with a message in, and maybe a photograph
of the type of cat you have ordered, and collect the real
animal after Christmas when all the fuss has died down and
the house is back to normal. You will stand a far better
chance of the cat settling in happily if you start this way, than
if it spends the first few days in your house being absolutely
terrified.

FAMILY PARTIES

The excitement, rushing around, moving of furniture and noise
which accompany a family party, especially a children's party,
are very unpleasant for a peace-loving cat. Add to this the
arrival of a whole number of guests or shouting children all
keen to play with the frightened animal, and you can see how
unhappy your cat could become if you didn't take steps to
protect it.

If at all possible, try to keep your cat outside or at least well
out of the way of the preparations. It is then less likely to pick
up any tension in the air from you, and it will not be under
your feet while furniture is being moved around and food
prepared. Ideally it should be allowed to roam around outside,
and so be undisturbed.

It is best to feed your cat well before the guests are due to
arrive, even if this is not its normal mealtime, so that it can
then go out again or curl up in a peaceful room well away from
the celebrations. (If the normal feeding time clashes with the
party time, your cat is unlikely to settle to eat then anyway, so
it is better to try to offer it food beforehand.)

Don't inflict lots of strangers on your cat at once, especially
if it is a kitten. They may well be keen to see the new arrival
(or even see how the old arrival is doing!) but your cat really
will not enjoy being shown to all these new people. It is better

to avoid this if you can, and making an excuse is better than having to apologise after your scared cat has refused to be handled and fled out of the room.

This is particularly true for children who may not have been taught how to approach or to handle a cat properly, and who can be over-boisterous. A mishandled cat may well scratch or bite, which will lead to tears and upset, and spoil the party atmosphere. It is far better to remember that 'parties and cats don't mix' and keep the guests away from your pet. If you do this then everyone (including your cat) will be happy.

APPENDIX

G.C.C.F.
4-6 Penel Orlieu
Bridgwater
Somerset
TA6 3PG
Tel: 01278 427575

Enquiries regarding bringing a cat into the U.K. from abroad to:
Imports Section
Ministry of Agriculture, Fisheries and Food
Government Buildings
Hook Rise South
Tolworth
Surbiton
Surrey
Tel: 0181 330 4411

Pets Pleasure
Crowland Street
Southport, Lancashire
PR9 7RZ
Tel: 01704 542147

INDEX

FREE

If you would like an up-to-date list of all **RIGHT WAY** titles currently available, please send a stamped self-addressed envelope to:

ELLIOT RIGHT WAY BOOKS, KINGSWOOD, SURREY, KT20 6TD, U.K.